February 5, 2011

Batter up!

[signature]

MEET THE REAL JOE BLACK

ENDORSEMENTS

"I'm honored to be his little brother because our lives are very, very similar."

—Bill Cosby

"In this book you will read about a man who grew up poor but lived his dreams with respect and dignity."

—Martha Jo Black (Daughter)

"We're going to have you share a room with Jackie Robinson and, if you're lucky, some of his competitive spirit will rub off on you."

—Dodger executive Spencer Harris

"Joe was tenacious and inspirational."

—Don Newcombe

D0898606

"*Joe Black's reservoir of information and passion for the game helped me put together a successful new baseball organization in 1998.*"

—Jerry Colangelo, owner of the Arizona Diamondbacks

"*What I respected about my friend Joe Black was his sense of fairness, integrity, and compassion.*"

—Joe Garagiola

"*Joe always wanted to help and did not seek credit or accolades.*"

—Dusty Baker

"*If heaven is home plate, Joe is safe at home.*"

—Joe Garagiola

"*Joe Black was unique in that he transcended all generations and societies.*"

—Dusty Baker

"*You're my friend then; you're my friend now.*"

—Sandy Koufax to Joe

"*He was one of the best, most fair, and strongest men that I know.*"

—Dusty Baker

Meet the Real Joe Black

✦

An Inspiring Life - Baseball, Teaching, Business, Giving

Steven Michael Selzer

Foreword by Bill Cosby

Introduction by Martha Jo Black

iUniverse, Inc.
New York   Bloomington

Meet the Real Joe Black

iUniverse books may be ordered through booksellers or by contacting:

iUniverse
1663 Liberty Drive
Bloomington, IN 47403
www.iuniverse.com
1-800-Authors (1-800-288-4677)

Because of the dynamic nature of the Internet, any Web addresses or links contained in this book may have changed since publication and may no longer be valid. The views expressed in this work are solely those of the author and do not necessarily reflect the views of the publisher, and the publisher hereby disclaims any responsibility for them.

ISBN: 978-1-4401-7119-2 (pbk)
ISBN: 978-1-4401-7120-8 (cloth)
ISBN: 978-1-4401-7121-5 (ebk)

Library of Congress Control Number: 2010901717

Printed in the United States of America

iUniverse rev. date: 5/10/2010

Contents

Foreword

A friendship with a man like Joe Black is not measured in terms of money, or the discounts he gave me to ride the Greyhound bus, or the boxes we would sit in for Major League Baseball games, or how often we would go down to Morgan State University and hang out with professors and faculty. A friendship with a man like Joe Black is measured in emotion.

In May 2002, my friend Joe was dying—prostate cancer gone unmanaged. I never visited the hospital room, because he was in Phoenix and I really didn't want to see him like that. He had lost his leg because the cancer had metastasized to his spine, his liver, and just about everywhere else now, and he was morphed up. When I would call, his daughter, Martha Jo Black, would pick up the phone. I would always begin with a comment that was a little offbeat, maybe even cruel in some people's eyes, but Joe and I knew what it meant between the two of us. We really didn't mean it—we were just being naughty. Joe Black. I'm his little brother, and I'm honored to be his little brother because our lives are very, very similar.

I can only think that most people in that much pain and on that much morphine—and so close to not having to make any decisions at all about living—would not be clear. But each time I'd call he was just as quick as always. And I knew I was giving him something he enjoyed, even in this moment when death was going around turning out the lights.

One time, after Martha handed Joe the phone, I said, "Hey man, I'm out at your house."

"Yeah," he said.

I said, "I'm in the backyard."

"Yeah," he said.

I said, "And I've dug up under the apple tree and I can't find where you hid the money."

"Wrong house," he said, and we just laughed.

Another such call would produce one of the most wonderful experiences in my life. Martha answered, as usual. I don't remember if Chico, Joe's son, was there. I had no idea how little time Joe had left.

"Hey," I said.

He said, "I want you to do me a favor—I want you to play the hot corner for me."

If you don't know what I'm talking about, Joe Black was a pitcher for the Brooklyn Dodgers. A great pitcher for the Dodgers. And so here's this great pitcher, saying he wants me to play third base for him. "I want you to play the hot corner for me." That means third base. That's the hot corner. Now, all my life, in the little bit of sandlot ball I played in a real uniform and borrowing someone else's glove, I stayed as far away from third base as possible. I'm an untaught, unskilled sandlot baseball player who never hit a home run. I hit a triple once because it went through the legs of an outfielder, and I hit a double once, which would have been a home run had it not been hit a foot to the left of the right field foul pole.

I said, "You got it."

He said, "The bases are drunk and I got two balls and no strikes."

I said, "Joe, I'm going to the hot corner, and I got a glove, and I just want you to know, Joe, that when he hits it to me I'm going to do something that I've never done in my life. When that ball comes screaming on the ground, a grass burner, I'm going to get down, put the glove down there, and I'm gonna look it in. Because I'm gonna tell you something, Joe—all my life, whenever someone hit the hot burner to me, I turned my head. But for you I'm gonna look it in."

"Let's go," he said.

He died about ten hours later. Yet, I must tell you that my eyes don't water when I think of this. I just think with great happiness of the memories, the wonderful memories, of a real friend who still lives with me. And that is why sometimes my wife is wrong when she hits me in the back of the head when I am sitting in a room with her and saying nothing—just smiling.

—William H. Cosby Jr., Ed.D.

Introduction

I have the honor of writing the introduction to this book. Mr. Steven Selzer was one of my father's students from his teaching years, and they maintained a mentor-mentee relationship for the rest of my father's life. In this book you will read about a man who grew up poor but lived out his dreams with respect and dignity. I hope you enjoy meeting the real Joe Black.

My father was my hero, my best friend, and my mentor. He taught me so much about life, showing me all different types of experiences and people. Some of these experiences were on a Major League Baseball field, during batting practice when I was a child. Others were at churches and various other places.

My father introduced me to his celebrity friends, but he always talked to me about people less fortunate, and we spoke often of their struggles. The main rule he taught me was that regardless of a person's financial wealth or fame, it is what is in the heart that matters.

Unfortunately, as many other young people have experienced, my parents divorced in the early 1970s, when I was five years old. My father fought for custody of me, not because of his ego or because he was trying to prove my mother was unfit as a parent, but because he felt in his heart that I needed guidance, support, and love. He actually spoiled me with the time, love, and support he gave me.

My father passed away in May of 2002, at age seventy-eight. It has taken this long for my heart to understand that my hero is not coming back to me. But at some point in life, we all have to learn to exist in a world where our fathers are gone.

Nellie Pike Randall wrote a poem that speaks of my relationship with my father.

"Every day of my life has been a gift from him. His lap had been my refuge from lightning and thunder. His arms had sheltered me from teenage heartbreak. His wisdom and understanding had sustained me as an adult."

This inspiring book teaches the importance of civility, character, and respect. It will give realistic hope to everyone who reads it. This book is about the man I am proud and honored to call my father, the real Joe Black.

—Martha Jo Black, 2010

Chapter 1
What Goes Around Comes Around

My late father, Nathan Selzer, owned an auto body shop in our town, Plainfield, New Jersey. As is always the case, the shop was located in the poorest neighborhood adjacent to the railroad tracks. The shop had a yard full of wrecked cars next to it. Right next to the yard was a very modest house where a family lived, the Black family, composed of two parents and six children. The children would often play outside and always greeted my father with a friendly smile and wave, which he would return.

One summer day, as my father was leaving work to go home, he spotted young Joe Black, age ten, throwing rocks against the front stoop of his house on East Fourth Street. This was a common activity for Joe, who greeted my father in the usual way. My father smiled back, but instead of waving, he raised his left arm and with a flipping motion tossed an object into the air toward Joe. The young boy followed the flight of what he could make out only as a white sphere. When it came down toward him, he instinctively caught it and stared at it for a moment. He realized that this was the first real baseball he had ever touched. Joe looked up to thank my father. Too late. Nathan Selzer was down the road.

Young Joe Black slept with that ball for a year. He went on to become a major league pitcher, Rookie of the Year in the National League, and the first black man ever to win a World Series game when he pitched the Brooklyn Dodgers to victory over the rival New York Yankees in the first game of the 1952 World Series. It was a dream come true for him. His roommate on the Brooklyn Dodgers, Jackie Robinson, became a good friend, as did his catcher, Roy Campanella, who had also been a teammate on the Baltimore Elite Giants in the Negro leagues.

Joe told me that story only about ten years ago. He wanted me to know since he figured my father had never told it to me, because my father wanted only to do good deeds, not to be acknowledged for them. That was my father's reputation, he said. It was true; my father had never told me or anyone, to the best of my knowledge, about Joe and the ball.

Chapter 2
In the Beginning

Joseph and Martha Black moved in the 1920s from the South to the North for the new day and the new jobs that were available in the more industrialized urban cities. They had heard of opportunities in factories instead of in fields. They had fifth- and sixth-grade educations, respectively. Their migration carried them to Plainfield, New Jersey, a small residential/industrial city located thirteen miles from Newark and twenty-four miles from New York City. In Plainfield, they raised six children—Ruby Elizabeth, Leola, Joseph Jr., Alvin, Phyllis, and Allean.

Mr. Black was an auto mechanic who had never been given the opportunity in the workplace to become a master at his trade. Because of prejudice, he could only find employment pumping gas or sweeping out service stations. Those work opportunities became so scarce that in 1934, the Black family survived only because of the National Relief Act, an early form of welfare.

Because of her limited education, Joe's mother helped support the family by taking in laundry and doing domestic work in the homes of several prominent white families. Both parents kept their disappointments to themselves and gave time to the family. Martha Black had only an elementary school education but was, according to her son Joe, "a heavyweight in mother wit and common sense." Joe's sister Phyllis, three years younger, noted that their mother had no book learning but was loaded with street and common sense. Chores were assigned to all the children, and they were constantly reminded to look out for and help one another. Joe commented later, "Household assignments were our early introduction to responsibility. And although we would mumble/grumble as we performed the tasks, we enjoyed doing them because they made us feel like necessary 'cogs' in the family."

When Martha Black came home from a hard day's work, she always took the time to ask each of the children, "What did they teach you in school today?" If any child sought the easy way out by saying, "Nothing," that child, Joe said, "Would have a stammering good time trying to explain how you can sit in a classroom for six hours and not learn anything."

The Plainfield school system had a practice at that time, whether intentional or not, of placing most black males in Industrial Arts and black females in Home Economics once they reached high school. Joe completed his first day in high school in a disgruntled mood. He had been assigned to auto mechanics, basic arithmetic, and industrial courses. He explained to his mother that he would probably fail some classes because he did not like the subjects. She said, "Let's go see the principal tomorrow."

Joe recounted what happened:

The next day I was embarrassed as I walked to school with my mother. My peers, friends, and strangers were looking at me with that all-knowing grin on their faces because a parent coming to school usually meant that you were in trouble.

We were invited into the principal's office, and he was

courteous, but not convincing, as he attempted to explain that I had been assigned shop classes to prepare me better for the work world, since in all probability I would not be going to college. Wow! He shouldn't have said that.

My mother stood up and maximized her five feet, eight inches and 180 pounds, looked the principal straight in the eyes, and pointed her finger as she told him, "Don't you tell me how poor we are, or what's gonna happen to my children—you just put Joe back in those classes with those rich kids, or it's going to be me and you."

The principal flushed, but he recognized that my mother meant business, and as he ushered us to the door, he said, "We'll see what we can do."

Needless to say, that was my last day as an Industrial Arts student. I was transferred to another tract, which included college preparatory courses.

That evening while we were having supper, my mother reminded us that she would always be there if we had a problem but not to let anyone make us feel inferior. "You ain't no better than anybody else," she said, "and ain't nobody better than you."

Joe's mother's words, which she repeated often, became a mantra of self-esteem. He never did have a problem with the other half of the equation. There was never even a hint of arrogance about Mr. Joe Black throughout a lifetime of successes and well-deserved prominence. He needed no reminders that we all are in this world together, and he felt we owed it to each other to be respectful. According to his sister Phyllis, he was a great believer in humility. She said they were all taught that "the Lord can take away what he gave you when you overdo."

Chapter 3
The Rocky Road to the Big Leagues

The route to Major League Baseball was long and arduous for Joe Black. At Plainfield High School, Joe had excelled after he developed as a player. He started out as a catcher. He explained why:

> Because my parents had limited spendable income, I told the coach that I was a catcher. You see, I didn't own a baseball glove, and the school provided the catcher's equipment, including a mitt. I tried to fudge it. I recall donning the catching equipment and convincing myself I would not blink when the batter swung at a pitch. I was asked to be the first catcher during batting practice. I squatted behind the plate and, if the pitch was within my range, I would catch it in the mitt. But, if it was to my right, I'd reach out and catch it with my bare hand. Other players gathered around the batting cage, laughing at my strange catching demonstration. After a few minutes, Coach Liddy asked me if I had ever caught before. Fortunately, Coach Liddy understood and taught the enthusiastic young man the fundamentals.

Young Joe made the junior varsity team. He would improve his game in the city's summer league. The director of the league, Mr. Vic Liske, and a former teacher of Joe's, in later years said, "Joe was completely gung-ho about baseball. Every morning he would help me with the equipment and on days when his team wasn't scheduled to play he would sit around hoping that one of the teams would need a substitute. His enthusiasm and love for baseball was really something else."

As a player, Joe had natural talent and could play most positions. In the Junior League, he had played third base, first base, and catcher. He had an outstanding arm and was a good hitter.

It was Joe's dedication to his beloved sport, baseball, that made him realize his fondest dream—becoming a Major Leaguer. Joe mentioned that among his memories about high school baseball is that he caught a glimpse of Albert Einstein when the team went to Princeton for a game. How many high school ballplayers would even take notice?

On a rare day when his father was able to see him play, he learned a very valuable lesson during the game. As he told it:

> This is not the best way to learn you are a real part of a group because it was as the result of a fight. We were leading Nutley High in the sixth inning and it was my good fortune to get on base via a hit. I tingled with excitement when I saw the coach flash the bunt sign to the next hitter.
>
> Sure, I was six feet and one hundred ninety pounds, but I believed that I was a speedster on the base paths.
>
> The batter bunted the ball towards third base; when the fielder threw it to first, I didn't break stride as I rounded second and 'motored' toward third. I slid safely into the bag, but I guess my momentum made me bang into the third baseman. As I was brushing the dirt from my uniform, the third baseman jumped

on my back; my teammate, Don Schmidt, who was coaching third, rushed over and pulled the player to the ground.

That was the signal for five minutes of pushing, pulling, and punching among the two teams. When calm was restored, the umpire threw Schmidt and the third baseman out of the game. Some may ask, what's the big deal? It's a big deal when you are the only black ballplayer on the field and your teammates go to "Duke City" to show you that we are a team.

In high school Joe did well academically. Learning took a commitment that his mother had ingrained in him. He was a star athlete in football and baseball and received several scholarship offers. He went all out both in academics and athletics. He did not believe in failure and playing Major League Baseball was his dream. Two of the players on the baseball team were signed by professional teams. Joe explained:

"During my senior year, I eagerly awaited baseball season. But my anxiety and joy turned to hatred, frustration, and a deep-rooted hurt. Yes, some members of the 1942 Plainfield High baseball team were signed by baseball scouts, but I wasn't one of them. A scout simply said: 'I'm sorry, Joe, but colored guys don't play in the Big Leagues.'"

Joe had never really thought about that issue up until this point in his young life. He thought the scout was joking. That night he went through his baseball scrapbook. Every face he looked at—Lou Gehrig, Mel Ott, Paul Waner—all the Major League Baseball players were white. Joe remembered shredding his book. He did keep one newspaper picture of his baseball hero, Detroit Tiger Hank Greenberg, hitting a long home run. That was all that was left of his scrapbook. His dream seemed to be shattered:

"At eighteen years of age I could not understand why I wasn't allowed to play America's number one pastime, baseball. My grandparents and parents were born in this country. I was born here. I attended school and saluted the flag as I pledged allegiance. I sang the National Anthem and later 'God Bless America.' Now, if that didn't make me an American, then what did?"

Joe's mother, Martha Black, noticed the change in Joe's attitude including his acting cold toward some white friends and acquaintances. She asked him about his behavior. "I explained that I was still mad because white people would not let me play in the World Series. My mother listened and then told me, 'Sonny (my nickname), I don't know what white folks you talking about, but it sure can't be those children you go to school with.'"

His mother's common sense reasoning made him realize he was not thinking properly. Gradually, he came out of his shell and enthusiastically played baseball on several racially mixed teams over the summer. He also got a job at a printing company, working the graveyard shift so he could play ball in the Twilight League.

Chapter 4
College, Interrupted by the Army

Joe Black made his family proud by attending Morgan State College (now University) in Baltimore in the fall of 1942. His entire family escorted him the three blocks from home to the railway station. His academic and athletic skills had earned a scholarship (actually a football scholarship, since Morgan had no baseball team, which was common at that time).

As he waited for the train, he was both proud and nervous. His mother was teary eyed. None of her children had ever left home before. She talked so she wouldn't cry.

"Sonny, we wish we could have given you lots of clothes to take with you, but you know we don't have a lot of money. Besides you're not going down there to be pretty. You're going to college to study and learn something. You listen to those teachers, 'cause I want to see some good report cards."

At Morgan State Joe did play football but he was a serious student. He made honorable mention All-Conference. He liked the motto of the 1942 team: "Be like the ivy on the wall, together cling or together fall."

One of the football coaches, Talmadge "Marse" Hill, taught Health Education as well. As a teacher in particular he gained Joe's respect and admiration because he spoke with eloquence and flair. Joe observed, "I'd sit in his classes and stare at him and silently wish that one day I could stand before an audience and articulate like him. That was a strange daydream for a man who was getting a C in Speech class because I couldn't stand in front of a class and talk. Also my vocabulary included youthful Jersey expressions such as 'Youse guys' and 'whatcha gonna do.'"

Years later, Joe Black was invited to be the guest speaker in 1974, when Morgan had its formal dedication of the Talmadge L. Hill Fieldhouse. This was a joyful event for Joe and was tremendously appreciated by Coach Hill, who sent Joe a letter which Joe treasured. A portion of the letter reads:

Dear Joe:

On Dedication Day, October 25, you provided me with the greatest thrill of my life. I was completely overwhelmed by your articulate and soul-stirring dedicatory address.

It was most thrilling to me because every word you uttered was filled with intense sincerity, glowing warmth, and indices of high reverence.

Among the myriad flow of graduates of our Alma Mater in the past four decades, you stand out as a living example of the high aspirations, high desires, and high hopes that every coach or instructor envisions.

Joe, you have wrought well. You have worn your cloak of fame modestly, and woven in and through the matrix of your garment shine the iridescent threads of dedication, determination, and devotion. Joe, I salute you as one of the most beloved scholar-athletes of my career.

/s/Talmadge L. Hill

Joe Black always remembered the importance of Morgan to his education and his life. He gave back to the University in many ways, not simply financially but of himself. Even after Joe's life ended, the benevolent Bill Cosby gave two concerts at Morgan to raise funds for scholarships in the name of his dear friend.

Just before his sophomore year at Morgan, Joe received a letter that read: "Greetings from the President of the United States." It was notification that he was being drafted into the Army for duty in World War II. He spent two and a half years in Army khaki before being honorably discharged in 1946. Joe performed all of his military stateside.

One matter of note is that Joe Black was introduced to alcoholic beverages in the Army. His buddies, upon hearing this, could not believe it and wanted to introduce him to drinking. They went on leave to a fancy club in New York City. His Army buds ordered a "Tom Collins" for Joe since it looked and tasted like lemonade, only hard. Joe told his friends it didn't taste bad and had four more before they got on the train at Penn Station to head back to their base on Long Island.

The next morning when Joe awoke he observed, "My stomach felt sore and it ached. In fact, my entire body seemed to be stiff and sore but I attributed it to my introduction to the consumption of alcoholic beverages. During breakfast, one of my buddies gave me a different reason. He greeted me with, 'Man, I didn't know you liked to fight so much.' When I looked at him quizzically, he said he was not joking and

that my last confrontation was with the M. P. at the gate to the base."
Sure enough, Joe found that several M. P.'s were waiting for him the
next night to settle the score.

"But that night I had a real talk with myself and admitted that I
could not control my conduct under the influence of alcohol. I would
not do any more drinking." He kept that promise to himself for the
rest of his life.

Once the Army stint was over, Joe returned to Morgan State where
he was a member of Omega Psi Phi fraternity. He proudly earned a
B.A. degree in Physical Education and Psychology which enabled him
to have a career in education, as one of his several careers. Joe Black
truly believed that knowledge was power and sought knowledge of all
kinds at every juncture of his life.

After that scout had told Joe that there were no black players in
the major leagues, Joe reflected, "I wouldn't admit that my dream was
dead—I just pushed it to the back of my mind." As Star Wars director
George Lucas once said, "Dreams are extremely important. You can't
do it unless you imagine it." Well, Joe imagined an integrated big
leagues where he would have a chance to show his talents which he
would work on developing.

Chapter 5
The Negro Leagues

"Baseball, considered by many to be America's number one pastime, has been a thriving recreational and employment aspect of this nation since 1839. Young men, black and white, could be seen cavorting on fields and in the streets as they endeavored to perfect their skills in catching, throwing, and hitting a baseball. It was exciting fun because many were hoping one day that they would be playing Major League Baseball. However, for one segment of the population, for many years this was an impossible dream. For many, many years those in power positions in baseball thought that skin pigmentation was more important than skill and deemed that Major League Baseball was for white males only."

Those are Joe Black's words, written in 2001 for the foreword of a book called *Black Baseball's National Showcase*, by Larry Lester. [i]

Since Major League Baseball had a "for whites only" policy at that time, black businessmen and sportsmen developed their own professional competition. In 1920 Rube Foster developed the Negro Major Leagues. In the summer of 1943, Joe Black and a friend from Morgan State went to Bugle Stadium, home of the Baltimore Elite Giants, a team in the National Negro League.

Once there, they introduced themselves as students from Morgan State College to Mr. Vernon Greene, owner of the team.   Joe and his friend told the owner they could really play.   He extended an invitation for them to come to the field the following Saturday and try out for the team.

Joe's friend decided not to try out for the professional Baltimore Elite Giants for fear of losing his amateur status and scholarship. That concern was quickly resolved since the C. I. A. A. did not identify baseball as a varsity sport.   There was no eligibility problem. Joe reported to the workout and performed well enough for Coach George Scales that he was invited to play in a game the next day.   He batted eighth and played shortstop.   At the plate he struck out four straight times.   He did the same the next day.

Coach Scales was losing his patience with Joe, who recalled him saying, "Where the hell did you play ball before? You couldn't hit a bull in the ass if it ran across the plate."

"Yes, I could," Joe retorted.   "Besides I never played baseball where catchers talked about poor control and watch your head."

"Aw, that's all talk, " Coach Scales uttered.   "The other teams are going to mess with you, you've got to learn to ignore it.   I really don't think you're going to make it.   Do you play any other position?"

Feeling a bit dejected, Joe replied in a hesitant voice, "I pitched back home in semi-pro baseball."

Coach Scales looked at Joe, turned to walk away but paused long enough to tell him to come back Tuesday night.

This is where Joe's determination and persistence showed themselves and allowed him to go on with a hopeful attitude.   Although his confidence was shaken, he would stay at it.

On that Tuesday night, Joe entered the clubhouse with some apprehension.   Coach Scales introduced him to Manager Felton Snow who had been in Chicago at the All-Star Game of the Negro leagues. The first thing the manager said to Joe was that Coach Scales and he had talked and that they were anxious to see Joe pitch. "So I'm going to start you tonight against the Black Yankees."

Joe recalled that, "A boyish grin came over my face and I uttered an inaudible thanks. 'Eggy' Clark, my catcher, was calling all of the right pitches, and I struck out the first six batters who faced me. Then, the bubble burst. Somebody must have brought in the fences because the batters were hitting my pitches against and over them. Scales came out to the mound and removed me with an unhappy grimace on his face."

Nevertheless, Joe Black persisted. He played against Josh Gibson, Buck Leonard, "Cool Papa" Bell, and many other legendary Negro leagues stars. While playing for the Elites, Joe remembered a game against the Homestead Grays. "Josh Gibson walked over to our dugout. He was big and looked super strong. 'Who's pitching?' he asked. After Manager Snow told him that Andy Porter was pitching, Josh walked over to Porter and said, 'You see this black bat, Porter? I'm going to hit you over that fence, that fence, and that fence.'"

Joe further commented, "Well, I don't know how many other times Josh had predicted home runs but this time he slammed balls over the centerfield and leftfield walls. His third home run effort bounced off the right field fence. And during my career in the National Negro League, I saw Josh perform other outstanding slugging feats. But Josh was more than a great hitter; he was a good base runner and a superb defensive catcher."

Even after Joe was drafted, and inducted into the Armed Forces on July 27, 1943, he managed to play part-time for the Baltimore Elite Giants because he was stationed in the New Jersey/New York area during his eighteen months in the Army. When he reported to the

Induction Center in Elizabeth, New Jersey, he met another New Jersey high school athlete, Larry Doby, who gained major league fame later. In fact, Joe Black much later led a successful campaign to get Larry Doby into the National Baseball Hall of Fame. Doby had been the second black player in the majors and, despite having better numbers than Jackie Robinson, he was passed over many times. Joe Black fought this injustice, and Larry Doby was finally inducted into the National Baseball Hall of Fame in 1998 while he was still living.

Roy Campanella joined the Baltimore Elite Giants in 1944. Campy turned out to be a teammate of Joe's on the Brooklyn Dodgers as well. Jim Gilliam, at age sixteen, became a star second baseman on the team and later on the Dodgers. As Joe stated it, "Hard work, discipline, and a strong desire to be one of the best carried Jim Gilliam from the role of a reserve to the heights of stardom. I repeat—his achievement was not quick or easy. Jim persuaded me many times to accompany him to Yankee Stadium or Ebbets Field so that he could observe the actions and mannerisms of the Big League second basemen."

Jim Gilliam became Joe's best friend on the team. Joe was six years older and much better educated than Gilliam, who did not finish high school. Joe noted about Jim, "In our early conversations he would say some things that made me realize that his athletic successes made him more conscious of his lack of educational preparation. Because of the rapport that existed between us, I could tell him that sports were not the only thing in life; he would have to broaden his awareness of the world and its happenings. No, he did not stop reading the sports pages, but he did begin to read the bold headlines on the front pages of newspapers. And soon he started reading the stories that went with the headlines. This helped to improve his self-confidence in his communications with new acquaintances or teammates. He learned to be a listener while he improved his vocabulary. Yes, Jim Gilliam educated himself, but the young athlete of today cannot successfully compete in today's changing society with Jim's limited formal education. Today's technological and scientific advancements mandate that people have educational or work skills beyond the high school level."

Joe was improving his pitching skills while facing the high level of competition in the National Negro League. In one game the Baltimore Elite Giants were playing against the Birmingham Barons in May of 1950. Joe had just graduated from Morgan State and was on the mound against a pal of his, Bill Greason. They had an agreement that they would not waste curveballs and throw each other only fastballs when the other was at bat. That meant they could take their home run swing every time, knowing the pitch would be a fastball. Joe went up against Greason for the first time that day. He described what happened:

Well, in the third inning I caught one of Greason's fastballs in my swing and the "slam" of the bat against the ball told me that I had given the ball a ride. While running to first base, I glanced at the ball in flight and noticed an outfielder racing toward the fence in left centerfield. I laughed to myself, because I knew that I had a double or triple, but when I rounded first base my grin turned to chagrin. The outfielder had caught my long drive and was throwing the ball to an infielder. While trotting back to our dugout, I mumbled some words under my breath. I sat next to Gilliam and asked, "Who the heck is that guy?"

Jim said, "That's Willie Mays, a young high school boy. Joe DiMaggio is his idol; that's why he wears number five. He can go get 'em. If it stays in the ballpark, Willie will catch it."

They say first impressions are lasting impressions, and for twenty-seven years I watched in admiration as Willie would go get 'em.

Black was the fastest of the pitchers on the Baltimore Elite Giants but year after year no white general managers cared. He had an overpowering fastball and a good curveball. It did not matter. The quota was too narrow. He observed, "If you want to get sad, I pitched my greatest games in miserable ball parks, in the Negro leagues, with no one watching." He is quick to add, "But I'm not a sad guy." Joe helped the Baltimore Elite Giants to win two championships in seven years.

While serving in the Armed Forces, Joe pitched quite a bit. He got to pitch to guys who were major leaguers. His base coach was Tommy Bridges, former All-Star pitcher with the Detroit Tigers. After the military, Joe played in the Winter Cuban League against top players. He pitched two years in Havana with the Cienfuegos Baseball Team. For the two seasons, Joe's record was 20-13. In fact, in the winter of 1953, he continued his winning ways with a 15-6 record (tops in the Winter League in wins) and a 2.42 ERA. He believed the Cuban League to be on a par with Triple-A baseball.

During his tenure in Havana, Joe Black had the opportunity to talk to Fidel Castro, who was a student in law school at the time. Castro had always liked and played baseball. On many occasions Joe saw him come to the stadium and watch the teams practice. According to Joe, "One day, Fidel Castro observed me warming up with Ray Noble, team catcher. After observing me pitch for about five minutes, he started to converse with me. Our conversation was in Spanish, but I'll relate it in English. Castro asked me why I was pitching from ten feet behind the 'rubber.' I explained to him that it stretched my muscles and helped me to improve my control. Castro looked at me and said, 'You're loco.'"

Chapter 6
A Step Closer to the Major Leagues

In 1950, an important cable reached Joe during his first winter season in Cuba. It was from Fresco Thompson, vice president of the Brooklyn Dodgers. "The contracts of Jim Gilliam and you have been purchased conditionally by our Montreal Royals farm team. You are expected to report to Vero Beach, Florida on March 9."

Gilliam and Black reported to Vero Beach and were told by Manager Bobby Bragan that they would report to Montreal after working out with the Dodgers' Ft. Worth team in the Texas League for ten days. Black and Gilliam were taken aback. As Joe related, "Our astonishment was based upon a form of fear. You see, we both knew that there weren't any black players in the Texas League, and we were not certain that we had the discipline or the intestinal fortitude to be the 'Jackie Robinson' of the Texas League."

All went well in Texas. They went on to Montreal, where Jackie Robinson had played. Both players made the 1951 Montreal Royals Baseball Club in the International League. "Buzzie" Bavasi, Dodgers' General Manager, came to Montreal to assess the talent. Gilliam and

Black were playing well and handling themselves with restraint. But that restraint was severely tested. Joe Black described it:

> We were in Buffalo playing the Triple-A farm club of the Cincinnati Reds. This contest with the Buffalo team was different, because it was the first league game where I heard racial insults.
>
> From about the third inning on, my ears heard such words as "niggers," "dumb niggers," and "monkeys and niggers all belong in Africa." I determined the area of the Buffalo dugout from where the words were emitted, but I could not detect the name-caller. In between innings, I asked Gilliam if he could see the race-hater. He said he could not.
>
> In the ninth inning, I laid down a sacrifice bunt, and as I was trotting from first base to our dugout, the Buffalo tormentor muttered something. I only heard the words "like your dumb mother." Those were fighting words, and it was the name-caller's misfortune that peripheral vision had enabled me to catch him with his mouth open. As I returned to the dugout, I kept my eyes on the prejudiced ballplayer.
>
> In the last half of the ninth inning, I retired the first two batters on a ground ball and a pop-fly. When I glanced into the Buffalo dugout, I noticed that the agitator had moved closer to the runway that took us to our respective dressing rooms. He was planning a quick exit and I realized that I had to make a quick dash to that dugout if I was going to head him off. But first I had to get the final out of the game. The count ran to 2-2. Toby Atwell, our catcher, signaled for a curve. I shook him off until he called for a fastball. The total strength of my arm and body was behind the fastball I hurled toward Toby's target. As I released the pitch, I started toward Buffalo's dugout; luckily

the batter did not swing, and I was crossing the first base foul line when I heard the umpire's call of "strike."

As I entered the Buffalo dugout, there were about eight players between me and my "target."

I excused myself and brushed past them. Finally, I was behind him. Frank Carswell, a ballplayer who had played in the Cuban League, was saying, 'I don't think that you should have been yelling those names at those colored guys.'

The tormentor replied, 'Ah! They're just a bunch of dumb niggers.'

I retorted, 'This nigger is going to kick your ass.'

He half turned and, when his eyes confirmed it was me, he ran up the steps where he reached the water cooler and pulled out an ice pick or something. Then he faced me and said, 'Come on, nigger!'

I accepted the challenge, throwing my glove at him, and as he ducked, I leaped up, grabbed him, and cocked my fist to deliver a hard punch. Before I could bring my fist forward, Gilliam had grabbed my arm and was shouting, 'No! No! You're not going to mess it up for us.'

Three weeks later, the Buffalo team was in Montreal for a three-game series. While Joe was getting into his uniform, Manager Walter Alston came over to his locker and asked that Joe follow him. When they walked out into the runway, Joe saw the name-calling player. Alston explained that the guy had come over to apologize. Joe recounted, "He extended his hand and told me he was sorry that he had called me those names and he now realized that colored guys deserved a chance to play in organized baseball. It wasn't easy eliminating my feelings of animosity toward him, but I accepted his apology."

Several years later, the tormentor had the opportunity to reiterate that he was sincere and genuine when he apologized to Joe for the racial slurs. In 1956, he and Joe were teammates on the Cincinnati Reds. Joe told the story:

> One day, my white teammates and I were discussing the pros and cons of black people boycotting the buses in Montgomery. The tormentor was rather adamant in support of the position taken by the black citizens of Montgomery. The Cincinnati catcher in the bullpen that day was a teammate of his in Buffalo, and he said, 'Hey, how come you are so understanding about colored people. I remember when you called Joe those ugly names and he was going to beat the daylights out of you.'
>
> After overcoming his embarrassment, the player responded, 'Yeah, but I was young and bull-headed then and didn't know any better. But I now realize that this country is supposed to give everybody a chance.'

Chapter 7
Meeting Jackie

Joe Black was invited to Spring Training in Vero Beach in 1952. He took a train and was met by the Dodgertown Bus. He recalled, "En route to the training camp, I mentally applauded the Dodgers for developing a facility where all the players could be fed and domiciled without being embarrassed by the mores of Florida's dual society."

The bus pulled up to the administrative offices. Joe noticed that two men were conversing at a distance. He recognized Dodger executive Spencer Harris but did not realize that the other man was Walter O'Malley, president of the Brooklyn Dodgers. Joe later became close to Mr. O'Malley and particularly to his son and successor, Peter O'Malley.

Just then, Spencer Harris came over to welcome Joe and wish him luck in his attempt to catch on with the "big club." Joe recalled that Mr. Harris said, "We're going to have you share a room with Jackie Robinson. If you're lucky, some of his competitive spirit will rub off on you."

Joe was shown his room. He put his bags on the floor, sat on a chair, and looked out the window at the fruit trees and baseball diamonds. He sat there thinking about where to put his belongings. "You see," Joe remembered, "I admired and respected Jackie Robinson, and as such, I thought I should wait to learn his preference of bed and dresser drawers. About fifteen minutes later Jackie walked into the room. I got out of the chair and extended my hand. 'Hello, I'm Joe Black,' I said.

"We shook hands and he responded, 'Hello, I'm Jackie Robinson.' As any other baseball fan would do, I stared at him. I then reminded him that we had met in 1946 in Montreal. He acknowledged that and said, 'So, you're one of the new pitchers?'" Jackie then asked about Joe's pitching performance in Montreal in 1951.

Joe replied, "It wasn't anything to write home about. My won-loss record was 11-12. I think the Dodgers invited me to camp because I was 15-6 in the Cuban Winter League."

As he asked Joe to sit down, Jackie remarked, "'Any pitcher who can win fifteen games in the Latin American Winter League must be good.'"

"Then Jackie sat on the edge of the bed and surprised me with his point blank question: 'Can you fight?'

"My male ego quickly defended my macho image, and in a boastful tone I said, 'Yeah, I can sling hands.'

"I guess my response was what he expected, because number 42 of the Dodgers smiled and told me that I was big enough to fight and everybody assumes black guys can fight—but we won't fight on the field.'

"Jackie Robinson knew that Manager Charlie Dressen and his coaches would teach me the on-the-field fundamentals of baseball, but he took the time to impress upon me the psychological changes that black ballplayers must endure, [Jackie] slowly, and with deliberation, informed me that some players, writers, and fans still retained attitudes of prejudice."

Jackie Robinson, the man who had broken the Major League Baseball color barrier five years before after being signed by Branch Rickey, went on to tell Joe, "We should always remember that we were there to prove that we can compete and play with them—that black and white can play together and be successful. And we will not let the rednecks aggravate us into failure. It's not as bad as it used to be, and in some cities the name-calling and throwing baseballs at us is worse than in others. Quite often it's the fans rather than the players. We can't allow those crazy sons of bitches to bother us. We have the ability to play, and we're going to show them that we're in baseball to stay."

Joe pointed out that Jackie "withstood the pressures of high and tight pitches, attempted spikings, a black cat tossed on the field, and shoes held high with the exclamation, 'Shine these shoes, boy.' Through the years, I have given a great deal of thought to the question: who else could have persevered under these conditions and been successful on the ball field? I get the same answer each time. No one!" Joe Black did not think any of the other excellent black players of that time "could have handled the insults without reacting physically or letting it have an adverse effect upon their playing ability. Jackie had the guts to absorb the nasty, degrading tactics of some narrow-minded people. The players of today don't have to 'turn the other cheek' as Jackie did."

Joe expressed the view to me that it was not all racial. The idea of some of the white players, who had become complacent as reserves, was to force Jackie to fight. Then no other blacks would come into the major leagues. It was not all about the color of Robinson's skin. It was economics. Why not chase competition away before it really started?

Joe would be Jackie's roommate for his entire time on the Dodgers and his friend for life. In fact, Joe was an enthusiastic supporter of the charitable Jackie Robinson Foundation, which does great work.

Here is what Joe had to say about Jackie: "Millions of sports fans know Jackie Robinson, the athlete. Baseball and the Dodgers gave me a chance to know Jackie Robinson, the man, the husband, the father. If a man has never been on the front lines during a war, he can't really describe the fear and nearness of death. And if you aren't Jackie Robinson, you can't really describe the hell associated with being a pioneer. He was a warrior who swallowed his ego so that his people could be part of America's number one pastime, baseball." Joe Black glorified Jackie Robinson for all these reasons.

On April 15, 2007, Major League Baseball had a national salute in remembrance of Jackie Robinson's first game in the majors on April 15, 1947, sixty years earlier. Players on all teams could wear Number 42 that day. The Commissioner of Baseball gave a special award to Rachel Robinson in recognition of her husband's contribution to the sport and to America.

In 1972, "pressured by his former Dodger teammate Joe Black to do something, anything, to honor Jackie Robinson on the twenty-fifth anniversary of his historic step into the major leagues, the office of the Commissioner of Baseball Bowie Kuhn invited Jackie to make the ceremonial throwing out of the first ball at Riverfront Stadium, Cincinnati, during the upcoming World Series," according to Arnold Rampersad in his biography, *Jackie Robinson*. [ii]   Robinson used the occasion to urge the major leagues to hire its first black manager. Jackie Robinson died ten days later, at age fifty-three, without seeing that first black manager, who was hired two years later in 1974 when the Cleveland Indians employed Frank Robinson. Six former athletes were pallbearers at Jackie Robinson's funeral. One was Bill Russell of the Boston Celtics, and the others were old Brooklyn Dodgers: Joe Black, Don Newcombe, Jim Gilliam, Pee Wee Reese, and Ralph Branca.

In fact, Joe had some similar experiences to those of Jackie when Joe came onto the team five years after Jackie. Arnold Rampersad recounted,

"When Joe Black entered a game in St. Louis, insults from certain Cardinals became so graphic that Robinson and (Manager) Dressen protested to the league about the rabid use of the term "nigger" linked to obscene and other demeaning terms. (The targets were only Black and Robinson.) When Eddie Stanky, managing St. Louis, dismissed the nasty language as typical baseball teasing, and the team president, Fred Saigh, brushed off the protest as "too much fuss over nothing," Robinson disagreed. Race baiting, he insisted, had no place in the game. "You'd think that after six years they would cut that stuff out," he said. "I thought I had proved that those names don't hurt my play a bit."

The Dodgers were in the thick of a tight pennant race in September 1952. Joe was often called upon in crucial late-inning situations to save the game. Here is an excerpt from an issue of the *Baltimore Afro-American* newspaper that month:

> Joe Black, working under threat of death at the hands of an unknown avenger, turned in his most dramatic, if not his most effective 'fireman' chore of the season. Called upon in the second inning, much earlier than is usually the case, the ex-Morgan College athlete strode the pathway from bullpen to pitching mound.
>
> Not one human in the park was ignorant of the tense drama that was unfolding as Black took the long walk from deep left field to the center of the diamond. All knew Joe last week had received an anonymous note threatening his life if he appeared in this crucial series against the Giants. But the big relief

star came through with an amazing display of courage as he promptly choked off a bases-loaded situation with one out, and then proceeded to hurl scoreless ball the rest of the way, protecting the 5-2 lead the Dodgers had when he entered the game.

Joe felt it was important to acknowledge that many white players from the South, and one in particular, played a positive role in integrating modern-day baseball. Joe expressed these thoughts as follows:

It is a known fact that some of the Dodgers believed in the doctrine of 'for whites only' to the extent that they signed and delivered a petition to Mr. Branch Rickey. However, on that same Dodger team, there was a white player from the South who agonized and analyzed within himself before making the decision about with whom he would, or would not, play ball. The young man had a task that was not easy.

All his life, he had been exposed to the doctrines of 'their kind' and 'white was right.' Furthermore, baseball was more than a hundred years old and no one had talked about integration, and some of the petition signers were his friends.

I do believe that baseball, the Dodgers, and the black ballplayers who became Dodgers are all grateful that Reese's Christian faith, belief in democracy, and compassion for his fellow man motivated him to take a negative attitude toward the petition and extend the hand of friendship to Jackie Robinson.

"Pee Wee" Reese was the team captain, a title that was befitting because he was a leader. I'm not alluding to "Rah! Rah!" talks to inspire his teammates. No, I'm referring to the many times that players would take their problems to "Pee Wee" and await his guidance.

"Pee Wee" played an important role in 1953 in soothing the tension and preventing a potential racial clash among the Dodgers when Jackie Robinson was moved to third base and Jim Gilliam was asserted in the lineup (at second base). Others may not agree, but I say desegregation among the Dodgers was a successful venture because of the three R's: Rickey, Robinson, and Reese.

Chapter 8
The Majors, Finally

Joe Black did not reach the major leagues until he was twenty-eight years old. It had nothing to do with ability. At the time he finished college at Morgan State University, the color barrier existed. Even when the Brooklyn Dodgers broke the racial barrier in 1947 with Jackie Robinson and the Cleveland Indians with Larry Doby, only a trickle of players came into the major leagues.

Larry Doby came up in the summer of 1947 as the first black player in the American League. He was a New Jersey high school contemporary of Joe Black's, excelling in football, basketball, track, and baseball. The two became close friends from an early age.

Joe Black recalled when Doby went straight from the Negro Leagues' Newark Eagles to the Indians, "He was introduced to his new Cleveland teammates by manager Lou Boudreau. The first ten players refused to shake his hand."

The number of black players in the majors was very limited. As a result, many worthy black players were fully or partially cheated out of major league careers. Joe Black never showed any bitterness toward this obvious injustice. And he demonstrated admirable restraint dealing with the racial slurs heaped upon him at many ballparks by players and fans alike. He was an expert in anger management, even back then. Several times, Joe had to be accompanied to the field by FBI agents due to death threats. He was always fearless and courageous.

The Korean War had claimed as a recruit Dodger pitcher Don Newcombe for a two-year stint. As Arnold Rampersad stated in his biography of Jackie Robinson, the Dodgers found a stellar pitching replacement in "Joe Black, a handsome, six-foot-two-inch player from Plainfield, New Jersey, formerly with the Baltimore Elite Giants of the Negro leagues, then with St. Paul and Montreal in the Dodger organization. A college man like Jack, Black was an alumnus of Morgan State with a degree in psychology and physical education."

In his fine book, *Praying for Gil Hodges*, Thomas Oliphant called Joe Black "a pitcher with a wicked fastball." He went on to further describe Black: "He was almost as imposing a figure as Don Newcombe and could throw just as hard."[iii]

In 1952 at his first spring training as a Dodger, Joe roomed with Jackie Robinson. On the first full day, Jackie rose early, showered, and dressed. He told Joe he would meet him in the clubhouse. As Joe showered and dressed, he suddenly felt nervous. He wondered why. He thought introspectively, "A year ago I was here with Montreal and believed I was as good as or better than most pitchers in camp and would earn a shot with the 'big club.' Well, opportunity was knocking and this was the wrong time to have doubts. Were my apprehensions the result of hearing the fallacious stereotype that Negroes would never be successful pitchers in the big leagues because they couldn't think? Somebody really wanted to keep 'colored guys' from the so-called glamorous positions because black quarterbacks had to overcome the same prejudiced mentality in professional football."

In a stroke of good fortune, Joe benefitted in his pitching career, both on the Baltimore Elite Giants and on the Brooklyn Dodgers, by pitching to Hall of Fame catcher Roy Campanella. Joe said, "As a member of the Baltimore Elite Giants, I received a great deal of support and guidance from Roy Campanella, who proved to be a friend by deed. Campy had 'warmed' me up a few times and told me that I had good control." That was a confidence booster for Joe, who described their routine: "Campy believed the road to success needed 'great' control. Each day, at the conclusion of our regular workout, Campy would send me out to the mound and he would squat behind the plate. For fifteen minutes each day, I would throw a pitch to one 'spot.' The 'target' would change each day, but I would have to 'pump' pitch after pitch to a particular 'spot.' It became monotonous but Campy kept reminding me that an error of two inches in location could make the difference between an out and a home run."

Roy Campanella and Joe Black, catcher and pitcher, would go fishing in their spare time. "While waiting for the fish to bite, Campy gave me his pitching strategy for each National League hitter. I especially remember him emphasizing that you defeated the Cardinals by getting Musial to bat without any runners on base; and Ralph Kiner was always looking for a 'breaking' pitch. The role of mentor suited Campanella, because he was a gregarious and unselfish person. It pleased him to see others do well in the game of baseball." Joe well understood this appreciation, because he wanted to see others do well in life. In fact, he spent his life helping and encouraging others to do better.

In spring training, the Dodgers would play teams from the American League as well. The Boston Red Sox came to Vero Beach to play the Dodgers on a day Joe would pitch.

When Ted Williams came to bat, I stared at the superstar. I was awe stricken. My first pitch was a fastball, low and away for a strike. And as Campy threw the ball back to me, I was thinking, "Gee, he really does squeeze his hands around the bat and looks the ball into the catcher's mitt—and then at the return throw to the pitcher. He never takes his eyes off the ball." And Campy signals for a fastball and swoosh! He takes for called strike two. I peered in at Campy and he signaled for me to throw a fastball low and outside the strike zone. Common sense told me to waste a pitch, as my catcher suggested, but my ego told me that Ted Williams was merely going through the motions today. Oh yes, I was going to give him a fastball, but it was going to be inside, about waist high. I put all my 220 pounds behind the pitch and was stunned when I heard Ted's bat make contact with my "hummer." Furillo was playing right field but the ball was hit so hard that all he could do was turn and hope the ball would carom off the wall in his direction. Ted Williams loped into second base with a stand-up double. Time was called, and during the suspension of play, Ted yelled, 'Hey, pitch, you're going to do okay. You've got a pretty good fastball.'

I smiled and replied, "Thanks! You just turned it around."

Joe reflected, "My showing off put me in a perilous position relative to making the ballclub. You see, the three pitchers who followed me into the game held the Red Sox scoreless. The lesson was clear: I was so busy trying to impress the fans that I failed to get myself in the proper frame of mind to pitch against the Red Sox." Campy worked on Joe's psyche, and he did better in his next outings. At that time, he could recall the words of boxing champion Joe Louis: "Joe, if you are lucky enough to make the Dodgers, keep your old friends, because they'll be around when you won't be playing baseball."

"When the season opened, the Dodgers started slowly in part because Campanella, for one, was mired in a prolonged slump, but also because Brooklyn had not yet discovered Joe Black," wrote Arnold Rampersad. He went on:

> At first, Black seemed not much more than mediocre. If his fastball was impressive, his curve ball seemed modest; he had damaged fingers on his right hand. And two pitches comprised his entire repertoire.

> But after Black pitched two excellent innings against the Cincinnati Reds in Brooklyn to bring his record to seven innings without giving up a run, Manager Charlie Dressen saw the light and announced that he would rely on Black for relief in the future. On June 1, when the rookie preserved a victory, the Dodgers also moved into first place for the first time in 1952.

With Campanella's help, Joe's strong work ethic and positive attitude, his ability as a pitcher ultimately came to the fore. He made the team and was the Dodgers' most valuable player that season, according to Manager Charlie Dressen. They would not have won the pennant but for his effective relief pitching. In fact, he was the winning pitcher of the game when the Dodgers clinched the pennant.

Joe Black won the National League Rookie of the Year award. It was very unusual for a relief pitcher to receive this accolade. Thomas Oliphant said, "For that one magical season, he was magnificent." Former Dodger pitcher Carl Erskine said, "Somehow he was just unhittable in 1952. All of us threw pretty hard in those days. But Joe could throw strikes on little corner pitches and pick you to death with his control."

Especially in those days it was much more prestigious to be a starting pitcher than a pitcher coming out of the bullpen. Joe remembered his first relief assignment: "The first time was in Chicago against the Cubs. I went an inning, and I reared back and fired and nobody touched me. Afterward Dizzy Dean showed up and said to Dressen, 'Hey, that big colored guy throws as hard as me.'"

Joe recalled when Manager Charlie Dressen started him in a ballgame for the first time. "And then at the end of the season, after I'd relieved forty-five times, Dressen gave me a start. It's a 2:30 game, and here it was 2:20 and I was still sitting in the dugout. 'Hey,' Dressen said. 'You're starting. How come you're not warming up?' I told him I wouldn't know what to do with ten minutes' warm-up. In the bullpen, I'd warm up with twenty throws. I took seven minutes."

He accepted his sudden fame and stardom with humility and grace. He was both confident and modest. Joe Black always remembered what legendary singer Nat "King" Cole told him: "Don't ever get so big that you can't stay down with the little people anymore." That comment reaffirmed his own view:

Did all the publicity and accolades give me a "big head"? Well, if a professional athlete tells you that he has never been excited or moved by the flattering stories and/or pictures about him in the newspapers or magazines, he is stretching the truth. Basking in the sunlight of national publicity and adulation gives one a feeling of importance and it takes a great effort to keep your feet on the ground. It is easy for a person to believe that he is "Mr. Big." Well, I did have my share of moments, thinking that the world was mine. However, during the "off-season," I would spend a great deal of my time in Plainfield, where I saw that my mother was still doing housework, my sisters and brother were working in factories, the house was still by the railroad tracks, and my friends were still "humping" to make it. The reality of the situation made me realize that I was lucky to have been pushed by my family and friends. I was not a "star."

In his rookie season in the National League, Joe had the opportunity to pitch to some baseball legends. He described pitching to Stan Musial.

> We were playing the St. Louis Cardinals, and Dressen had waited for them to load the bases before calling me into the game. I threw my six warm-up pitches and prepared to pitch to Stan "The Man" Musial. Gil Hodges trotted to the mound from first base and asked for the ball. As he squeezed "the pill" in his massive hands, he wanted to know if I remembered how to pitch to "The Man."
>
> I answered, "Yep! Keep fastballs down and away and jam him with the breaking pitch."
>
> Hodges smiled and said, "That sounds right, but if I was pitching, I'd call time out, ask for a bucket of water, and I'd swallow this 'pill.'" Gil laughed, tossed the ball to me, and jogged back to his position.
>
> When Musial came to bat three innings later, the situation developed into a mood that was the opposite of the humorous effort by Hodges. As Musial stepped in the batter's box, a voice in the Cardinals' dugout shouted, "Hey! Stan, with that big, black background, you shouldn't have trouble hitting that white ball."
>
> I backed off the rubber and glared into their dugout, where I saw only blank stares and silence. Jackie rushed to the

mound and inquired if I had detected the name-caller. After my response, he said, "The gutless bastards always hide. Forget it right now and work on Musial."

Jackie returned to second base and I turned to pitch to "The Man." Campy signaled for a change-up and Musial flied out to short-centerfield.

In old Sportsman Park, the visiting team had to walk through the Cardinals' dugout to get on the ballfield. So, the next night as I walked through the dugout, Musial stopped me and explained, "I'm sorry that it happened, but don't let things like that bother you. You're a good pitcher."

Joe continued:

The memory of Musial's actions brings to mind the fact that 'back in the good old days' the stars of baseball did not allow their achievements to negate the development of a rapport with the fans. They always had time to sign an autograph, or say hello. It was the bench-warmers who usually were too important to share a friendly moment with a fan. But those bench-warmers sure worked overtime heckling us black ballplayers. It is my belief that we were perceived as a threat to their job security.

You see, through the years those guys had it made. They went to spring training, exerted a little hustle, and didn't make any waves, and those actions allowed them to retain the prestigious identity of being Major League ballplayers. Suddenly, there was a new guy on the block. The "humpties," or "bench-jockeys" were struggling to retain their status, while the black athlete had the strong motivation of dreams deferred, pride, and the hope that we would be the catalyst to a better tomorrow for some younger blacks.

Joe Black had only one outstanding year as a major leaguer, his rookie year. In 1952, Joe Black appeared in 57 of the Dodgers' 154 games. He won 15, lost 4, saved 15 games, and had an earned run average of 2.14. His excellent pitching propelled the Dodgers to the National League pennant. As stated, Joe Black won the Rookie of the Year award in the National League.

Even though Joe was a relief pitcher, Manager Charlie Dressen gave him the honor of starting the first game of the World Series against the New York Yankees. After starting only two games the whole season, he was going to start the first game of the World Series. The headlines in the New York papers read, "BLACK TO OPEN SERIES FOR BUMS."

"I had no idea that morning I was going to do something special. I was going out to pitch a game. I'd pitched a lot of games. I beat Allie Reynolds 4-2, and when I got the last out, they all came around. Reese, Hodges, Robinson—they're all slapping me on the back. Then it hit me. I didn't worry about a thing before, but going back to the clubhouse, I'm all butterflies."

Before that first World Series game, Joe noted that Pee Wee Reese, Duke Snider, Carl Furillo, Jackie, and Campy gathered around his locker to give encouragement before the big game. He then went out to face Mickey Mantle, Yogi Berra, and the rest of the Yankees. Joe said that while he was warming up he actually thought about the fictitious World Series he had pitched many times with those rocks against his stoop on East Fourth Street in Plainfield during his boyhood. Just as he always won that mythical game, he defeated the powerful Yankees by a score of 4-2 on October 1, 1952, becoming the first black pitcher ever to win a World Series game.

It is an interesting sidelight that Joe's sister Phyllis attended that game. She had been a loyal Yankee fan for years. After the game, Joe kidded her, "Well, I beat your boys today. I hope you're not upset."

Phyllis smiled and replied, "No, today I was a Joe Black fan."

Joe's mother Martha attended the game as well; she sat in the stands but could not watch. That is and has always been a mother's prerogative.

Joe started the fourth and seventh games of the World Series, pitched well, and compiled a low 2.53 ERA for the Series. It took seven games, but as usual, the New York Yankees won the World Series. Joe arrived at all the games of the World Series with an FBI escort because of death threats against him.

During his rookie year, Joe would seek advice from Red Barber, the Dodgers' storied broadcaster. Larry King, in his book, *Why I Love Baseball*, said, "As a kid I would listen (on the radio) to Red Barber and I swear I could see the game. His descriptions, down to minute details, in that wonderful Southern twang, became as much a part of Brooklyn as Coney Island."[iv]

One time, Joe Black and Red Barber talked about the baseball phenomenon known as the "sophomore jinx." The idea was to help Joe avoid unfounded mental pressures in his second year. They reached certain conclusions about potential mental roadblocks to continued success. These were:

1. Egotism (believing you have the game "whipped" and as a result subconsciously fail to project the same desire and effort).

2. Overextension of physical capabilities (trying to add or do things beyond your physical capacity).

3. Loss of confidence (failure to accept or adjust to failures that occur early during your second season).

Joe reflected later, "So what happened to Joe Black—big man in the bullpen in '52, journeyman in '53?   My record was 6-3 and an ERA of 3-plus in '53; it was a winning record but my pitching performance seemed mediocre when compared to my previous season, it goes without saying that no athlete wants to be a 'one-year flash.' It has bothered me through the years not knowing if the circumstances and events curtailed my effectiveness or if, like a meteor, I was just a temporary flash."

Joe's stagnation came despite the fact that, according to Don Newcombe, "Joe was the hardest working player on the team."

In retrospect, it does seem clear the overextension of Joe's physical capabilities was the reason for his decline as a pitcher in the major leagues. An examination of a newspaper column by Sportswriter Frank Eck in the September 27, 1952, issue of the Paterson (N.J.) Evening News is instructive:

Dressen first saw Black in the Spring Training (1952) at Vero Beach, Florida. He liked two things about Black. They were his size—all the way down to his long fingers—and the fact that he had played for Coach Billy Herman's Cienfuegos team in Havana.

"At first Black pitched like he was scared, but I got to use him a lot. His control and his fastball impressed me the more he pitched. When I noticed his long fingers, I tried to teach him another pitch. I'll get one for him yet. He's been getting by on two pitches—fastball and curve. But what control!" Charlie Dressen was saying.

"And true to his word, Dressen did try to teach me a new pitch," Joe said. "Spring training of '53 was not like '52, when I spent many hours working on my control and follow-through. It was impressed upon me that I had a great year in 1952, but I would have to get another pitch if I were to continue my winning ways."

There was one bit of friendly advice Joe recalled that was contrary to the manager's wishes. Pitcher Don Newcombe, or "Newk," told Joe, "Don't let them mess with your pitching style." Newcombe urged Joe to stay with what got him to the Dodgers.

Joe remembered, "All my instincts were telling me to walk away from this great experiment, but I realized that a negative attitude would project the image that I had developed a "big head" and would not accept constructive criticism. I was caught between the proverbial "rock and a hard place." Ultimately, popularity was the victor over my common sense, and I went along with the program of 'making me a better pitcher.'"

Spring training of 1953 should have been a pleasant, positive time, but it turned out to be a struggle that would affect the rest of Joe Black's career as a pitcher in the major leagues. It was a pivotal period in his life. He was, as usual, in great physical condition. His training consisted of endless running so that his legs would be strong and his endurance high. He further described that 1953 spring training:

> My time was used trying to throw: knuckle-balls, fork-balls, sinkers, and change-of-paces off my fastball and curve. My deformed index finger (from birth) negated my gripping the

ball properly when making an effort to throw these pitches and make the ball move on the correct trajectory.

In an effort to compensate for this problem, we tried adjusting my "stride." Sometimes I would lengthen my stride; other times I would shorten the stride; or stride more toward first base when trying to make the ball sink; or pitch across my body to slow the velocity of my curveball.

The undertaking was more comical than practical. Most of the time when I tried to throw the "new" pitches, I would throw the ball over the catcher's head or bounce it halfway to home plate. For weeks I strived to master a new pitch but Dressen's patience soon reached the point of no return, and he instructed me to go back to my old style. However, the trials and tribulations of different strides and pitches had deprived me of my former pitching rhythm and form. I would warm up ten feet behind the rubber or on the rubber but I didn't seem to have dexterity. It felt as though I was slinging rather than pitching the ball. I became flustered because of this strange turn of events.

I reached out for help by asking questions about my pitching style in 1952. Pee Wee Reese told me that it looked as though I would raise up my toes just before pivoting to release the ball. Jackie Robinson said, 'In your windup, you sort of hunched your shoulders.' Roy Campanella explained that in my pivot, I used to turn more of my back to the hitters.

Joe felt he was just going through the motions as the 1953 season began and as it progressed. Manager Dressen gave him many pitching opportunities in the hopes that he would return to his form of the previous season. "My teammates may have looked at me with pity, but none of them uttered negative criticisms in my presence. But I just could not find the real me, and my pitching was hurting the team."

Joe was demoted so that he no longer came into the game when it was on the line. He was now a pitcher who had lost both his control and his confidence. He said,

"In 1952, I intimidated some batters, but now those same players were using me for batting practice. Baseball was a job but it ceased being fun. An oddity of my pitching frustration involved Joe Garagiola. In '52, Joe was a catcher with the Pittsburgh Pirates, and most of the time I would dominate their hitters. Kiner, Bell, Westlake, and Murtaugh did not pop me like Garagiola. Although Joe Garagiola batted less than .270 in 1952, I think he batted .360 against me. But in 1953, when I was struggling, Joe was the one hitter whom I dominated. Perhaps he felt sorry for me."

Joe made an interesting and significant observation about this difficult time:

My disappointing mound appearances gave me an opportunity to see that the bond of respect and friendship was stronger than the competition between opposing teams. Players on other teams tried to help me during my trying times. Cincinnati's Ted Kluszewski told me, "Joe, you used to make the batters hit down on the ball, but now they are able to get under it and get good wood on the ball. Your pitches are about two inches higher." On another occasion, Warren Spahn and Lew Burdette sat with me in the outfield of Milwaukee County Stadium and discussed my plight. They emphasized that somehow I had changed my motion so it wasn't as smooth as last year. They urged me to show more confidence.

In a game against the Giants, I was pitching as though I had regained my winning form. During the game I got a base hit and, while holding me close to the bag, Giants' first baseman Whitey Lockman said, "Hey! You got it today. You're looking like the Joe Black of last year. Keep it up."

Peter Golenbock, in his book, *Bums: An Oral History of the Brooklyn Dodgers*, described what happened after Joe Black's first successful year on the Dodgers,

"And then the next year Charlie Dressen ruined him. Dressen had demanded that Black learn a third pitch, a big-breaking curve or screwball, forkball, or a change-up. But Black was born with stretched tendons on his index and middle fingers of his pitching hand, and physically he could only throw what he threw. By April Black's confidence was shot, and so was his control. His fastball sailed high, his curve ball bounced into the dirt, and the next year Clem Labine replaced Black as the top man in the bullpen. In '54 Black won no games, and in '55 he was gone from Brooklyn."ᵛ

Golenbock added the following thought: "And yet Joe Black remained a gracious and grateful man. At the end of his superstar '52 season, he presented each of the nine reporters who covered the team with a bottle of champagne in gratitude for their kind words."

In 1955, Joe was traded from the Dodgers to the Cincinnati Reds at mid-season. That was the year that the Dodgers finally defeated the Yankees and won their first and only World Series in Brooklyn. He missed out. Joe never complained about that major piece of bad luck and he always maintained a positive attitude. Dusty Baker said that it had to be real culture shock for Joe to go to Cincinnati in those days. He added that one of Joe's great attributes was his adaptability. "He was always proactive and not reactive," Dusty said. Joe would move on things and not wait. He would make the best of the situation.

Joe played in 1956 for the Reds. It was in Cincinnati that he met and befriended the young Frank Robinson. Joe broke Frank into the majors. Robinson had a tremendous career both as a Hall of Fame player for the Reds and the Orioles and as a manager for several teams. The two would develop a close lifelong friendship.

After the season, Joe's contract was sold to the Seattle Rainiers of the Pacific Coast League. In spring training, he warmed up and then threw a fastball to the catcher. Something happened to his arm, and the ball bounced ten feet short of the plate. The next pitch hit the ground several feet in front of the catcher. Joe was concerned and spent the next few days at camp running, exercising, and playing "pepper" games. He refrained from pitching. "However," Joe recounted, "as Joe Louis once told an opponent, 'You can run, but you can't hide.' The fear of throwing made me realize that I had to learn about the condition of my arm."

Joe went to the nearest VA Hospital as an outpatient. Some X-rays were taken of his arm, and the news was not good—there were floating chips in his right elbow and a small crack was developing in his humerus. "Man! How was I going to get back to the 'Biggies' with an ailing 'hose'?" Joe said. "I made a foolish decision; I opted to remain silent and hoped that I could use my head to fool opposing batters."

The Pacific Coast League batters pounded Joe's pitches. "Manager Lefty O'Doul was really patient as he endured my ineptness but I soon reached the point of no return. Lefty asked if I had a sore arm." When Joe replied, Lefty suggested that Joe should let them send him to Tulsa of the Texas League, where the sun's heat might help the ailing arm.

At Tulsa, the sun and some rest did have some positive results. "Subsequently my pitching did improve but it seemed as though my pitches would lose velocity after five innings. Pride, and probably the desire to beat them to the punch, made me accept the manager's suggestion that I should consider 'walking away' from the game. I did not have to sell the general manager into giving me my release. The air was rapidly escaping from my 'daydream of baseball longevity.'"

Joe took a long train ride home to Penn Station in New York. He spent the time reminiscing and sleeping. He then took a taxi to the family apartment in Brooklyn. He enjoyed his family time. He loafed around the apartment for a week and then started thinking about job hunting. An item in the newspaper caught his attention: "Cookie Lavagetto Named Manager of Senators." He had not thrown a baseball in two weeks. "So the next day, I telephoned Cookie and asked if he could use another arm. We spent a few moments chitchatting before Cookie told me to come to Washington during the weekend." Joe knew Lavagetto through the Dodger organization where he had been a coach with the 1952 Dodger team.

Lavagetto met Joe on the field at Griffith Stadium in Washington, D.C. that Friday. The manager asked the clubhouse man to issue Joe a uniform. "I dressed and trotted to the outfield, where I joined the other pitchers, who were shagging balls during batting practice. Pedro Ramos, one of the Senators' pitching stars, approached and challenged me to a foot race. Ramos liked to believe he was the swiftest runner on the ball team. I smiled and conceded defeat. My mind wasn't on racing. I was wondering if I would feel pain when I tried to pitch."

Cookie called Joe over to loosen up. Catcher Clint Courtney, who was American League Rookie of the Year when Joe won the award in the National League, squatted behind the plate. After a while Joe cranked it up. There was no pain. Joe observed what he saw. He elucidated:

"The ball popping into the mitt had caused some of the Senators to gather around. I felt confident and good, so I was eager when I was asked to demonstrate my 'funny little curve.' Some of the players 'oohed' as my pitches swooshed over the outside corner of the plate."

The next day team owner Calvin Griffith accompanied Cookie and Courtney to the bullpen for a final "look-see." Again the fastball was smoking and the curve was snipping corners. About ten minutes later, Mr. Griffith told me to come to his office after I had showered. Thus, Joe Black became the first black American to sign a contract with the Washington Senators Baseball Club.

Summing up his time with the Washington Senators, Joe said: "My tenure with the Senators was an enjoyable experience. The team didn't win too many games but they were a great group of guys. Roy Sievers led the league in home runs, Ted Abernathy was one of the top relievers, and the bats of Bob Allison and Harmon Killebrew made it evident that the Senators would score runs for many years."

While Joe was with the Senators, he got to pitch against American League batters for the first time (other than in the World Series). One of these batters was Moose Skowron of the New York Yankees. Joe's very dear friend, Chicago White Sox Chairman Jerry Reinsdorf was talking to Skowron well after he had retired from the major leagues. The topic was batting slumps. Moose indicated that the worst slump he had ever experienced was when he hit 0 for 41, then got a hit off Joe Black, and then went 0 for 20. Jerry could not wait to kid Joe about that sole hit in the middle of a bad slump when they next got together. As soon as Jerry mentioned it, Joe said it was a high fastball. Joe Black was blessed with a great memory.

Back to the Washington Senators, Joe recalled:

It's strange, but the day after I signed my contract, the pain returned to my arm. I remember pitching to Al Kaline. I took my windup and cut loose with what was supposed to be a "hummer," but pain slowed it down to a change of pace. Kaline took the pitch for a called strike, but I could tell from his reaction that he had heard that I threw "smoke." My next pitch was a ball, and Kaline backed out of the batter's box, looked at me, rubbed dirt on his hands, stepped into the batter's box, and then spread his legs "à la Joe DiMaggio." Kaline carried my next pitch into the leftfield seats of Briggs Stadium. That was the last home run hit off me in the Major Leagues.

Joe went on a barnstorming trip in the fall of 1957 with some of the black ballplayers. They went to Texas, Mexico, the Dominican Republic, and Panama. While in Waco, Texas, a few players decided to go to a movie. Joe related the story:

> When we arrived at the movie theater, I told the guys that I wasn't going to sit in the balcony. They laughed, told me that I was crazy. I took the dare and walked to the front entrance (rather than the side entrance) and purchased my ticket. When I reached the usher who collected the tickets, he stopped me with these words:

> "Sorry, but you have to go to the balcony."
> I looked at him and asked, "Que dice?"
> The usher repeated his directive, and I responded, "'No entiende! No speaky ingles."
> A perplexed look came upon the face of the usher, and he called for the girl behind the refreshment counter. The young Mexican lass came over and listened as the usher explained the situation to her.

The girl turned to me and asked, "Adonde nacieron?"

My reply was quick and brief: "Yo soy Cubano."

While she was explaining to the usher that I said I was Cuban, another gentleman joined us. He was the theater manager. He listened to the details of the predicament and then made his decision:

"He looks like a nigger to me, but if he's a Cuban, let him sit down here."

It took a great deal of self-discipline not to grin or laugh, so with a somber face I walked into the theater and sat among the sea of white faces. I sat and watched the movie as curious white faces sneaked looks in my direction. My mind repeated one thought: What really makes them think that skin pigmentation makes them better than a black person? Occasionally, I would sneak a peek up to the balcony and one of my cronies would wave, but I didn't dare wave back. My objective had been accomplished; (these) white Americans disliked black Americans, not the skin pigmentation. With an attitude of contempt, I left the "for white only" seats and joined my friends in the balcony.

He continued:

Sometimes I would travel on the bus with the Negro League All-Stars. This gave me an opportunity to spend some time with old friends. The players entertained themselves through conversation, card playing, and/or singing. But there was one player who sang more like a cowboy than a black man with rhythm. Once in a while we would ask him why he didn't sing the blues, like B. B. King, rather than make those Twang! Twang! country sounds. The player would smile and acknowledge that he knew the sound was different but he liked singing western songs. Several years later, I was buying records that this player had recorded. His dream of becoming a big league ballplayer didn't become a reality but Charley Pride became a superstar in the world of county and western music.

Joe commented:

The 1957 barnstorming sojourn ended in early November. Although I was wishing for an extended career, my inner self knew that my Major League career had come to an end. It was a gut feeling that I kept to myself.

In December 1957, I received my 1958 contract from the Washington Senators. But instead of signing it, I sat down and wrote a letter to Calvin Griffith, president of the Washington Senators. My correspondence informed him that the pain in my arm would not permit me to continue in professional baseball; thus, he should place me on the voluntary retired list or give me an unconditional release.

My letter writing was not a magnanimous gesture; it was an honest appraisal. I knew that I wouldn't consent to surgery and neither my arm nor my psyche could endure the constant fortification of cortisone shots. At the time I did not realize the finality of my act.

Two weeks later Joe was working out at the Harlem YMCA with Willie Mays and Jim Gilliam. After the workout, they recalled some barnstorming trips they had made together. When talking about the most recent one, Joe informed them that those games would be the last of his professional baseball career. "Jim asked me what did I mean? I informed them that I had returned my contract to the Senators unsigned and with a note that I was retiring from the game. They both expressed surprise because during the barnstorming trip I had pitched several low-hit games.

"That was a fact but to perform effectively I would visit doctors during the day and get a cortisone shot. My friends understood where I was coming from when I stated that I couldn't live with the pain and I couldn't endure constant medication."

In the fall of 1957, Bob Cook, Sports Editor of the *New York Tribune*, wrote a column that read:

The retirement of Joe Black who was released outright by Washington brought back memories bright and tragic. As one of the great relief pitchers of the day, Joe was with us only a short while and maybe some would object to the word "great" when it is applied to his name. But the members of the '52 Dodgers will be the last to resent it; they owe a pennant to the tall tower of instant relief.

Black was one of those pitchers who come along every so often with no ballyhoo, no Big League references, no letter of credit; he stepped from out of nowhere to enjoy his finest hour and then he was gone before you could say "Joe Black." Joe requested his unconditional release from Calvin Griffith just a few days ago. He had been barnstorming with a team, led by Willie Mays, this fall and it was during this tour that the pain in the arm removed all hope of continuing in the Big Leagues. At 33 he is calling it a career.

According to Manager Charlie Dressen's count, Joe Black won 27 games for Brooklyn in '52; he was officially credited with 15 and he saved 12 more. The next year he won 6, lost 3, and then was shipped to Montreal. He returned to the Majors for a final fling with Washington last summer.

He'll be missed by the baseball writers because they loved him in the press box; he had a quality of being genuine which stuck with the writers and sometimes you'd hear them cheering when Joe began to play. Perhaps it was the way Joe acted in his first interview which endeared him to the baseball writers. He was asked about his various pitches; what he threw; what were his specialties.

'Well,' said Black, 'I got a fastball, a change of pace, and that little curve of mine.' So, Joe Black won't be around next spring when the teams go south.

Roger Kahn, in his legendary book, *The Boys of Summer*, summed up Joe Black's major league career in this way: "Irony ringed Joe Black's life in baseball. He appeared without acclaim, determined and fearless, and quickly became the strongest pitcher on the team. Then, with success, came dread. These afternoons as a hero might vanish as suddenly as they had come. He had longed to succeed. Now nightmares warned of a sudden end. All of Joe Black's dreams came true, the good ones and the bad. Five years after his brilliant Dodger season, his baseball skill was spent. At thirty-three, he would have to make a new life and find another dream."[vi]

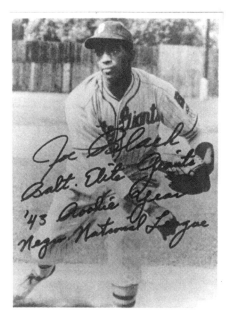

Joe as National Negro League rookie in 1943 - Baltimore Elite Giants

Joe pitching for the Brooklyn Dodgers - 1952

Coming Off Relief Role. Joe Black, Dodger relief specialist, who'll wake with a start tomorrow, wears tooth-paste-ad smile as he strolls past group of Yankees at Stadium yesterday. The lolling Yanks are (starting at left) Tom Gorman, Bob Kuzava, Jim Turner, Ewell Blackwell (hand to cap), Johnny Sain (behind Blackwell), Joe Ostrowski, Bill Dickey, Ray Scarborough and Vic Raschi. Joe will face Allie Reynolds in World Series inaugural at Ebbets Field. *Story a 5e*

(By Associated Press)

Joe and the Yankees 1952

59

1952 National League Champion Brooklyn Dodgers – Joe is in top row, far right. Others pictured are Jackie Robinson, Duke Snider, Gil Hodges, Roy Campanella, Pee Wee Reese.

Joe on the mound for Brooklyn Dodgers

Joe on the Cincinnati Reds - 1956

As a school teacher - Hubbard Junior High School, Plainfield, New Jersey

Coach Black's baseball team. Author is in second row, third from right

Joe as Vice President of Greyhound

Television interview - Greyhound Scholarship Program

"D.C. Salutes Joe Black Night" Statler Hilton, 1976;
Author is at the left end of the table next to Jesse Owens.
also pictured Martha Jo Black, Chico Black, Phyllis Greer

Joe and Bill Cosby

Joe and Andrew Young

Joe receiving Martin Luther King Distinguished Service
Award from Ms. Coretta Scott King – 1987

Willie Mays, Mickey Mantle, and Joe

Chapter 9
The Next Dream—Teaching That Counted

When his major league career ended in just a few years, Joe Black was pleased that he had been a good student and had a college degree that enabled him to teach. Mr. Black had an offer of employment that would have paid him three times a public school teacher's salary. A well-known company that produced alcoholic beverages wanted to give him a highly-paid executive position at their headquarters in central New Jersey. He turned them down for three reasons:

1. He was a teetotaler. He did not drink, did not want to begin, and did not want to appear to endorse alcoholic beverages.

2. Joe Black did not want to have to go to events for the company and drink and make small talk with folks. He did not envision using his talent for articulate, intelligent conversation in this way.

3. The most important reason of all: he was proud of the education he had received, which qualified him to teach and have an impact on young minds.

Joe Black proudly sought a teaching position in his hometown of Plainfield, New Jersey. "I wanted to use the mind that God gave me for thinking," he said. "I remembered that I had something no one could ever take from me—a college education." He was already a sports hero. He had used his intellect wisely and had studied hard in college. Athletics may have opened the door for him to secure a college degree, but he maximized this opportunity to learn.

Mr. Black gave his mother the credit for stressing the importance of education. She propped him up while he was growing up in poverty by constantly telling him, "Ain't nobody better than you." His mother, Martha Black, was an intelligent woman who, due to lack of educational opportunity, cleaned houses to help support the family even as Joe's father, a bright man, was forced to do unskilled labor.

In order to seek a teaching position, Joe took his degree from Morgan, along with his transcript, and went to the Plainfield Board of Education building.

Joe explained:

The Superintendent of the Plainfield School System, Dr. Victor Podesta, was a high school teacher and assistant coach when I was a student at Plainfield High. I wasn't approaching a stranger. He had always been a person with compassion and the ability to listen, so he was attentive as I articulated that I had had my "day in the sun" with sports and now was hoping to start a new career as a teacher. My timing was right. A teacher had submitted his resignation the previous week. Dr. Podesta smiled and said, "Joe, if you're really finished with baseball I think that you can be a valuable addition to our school system. Our students will be exposed to a graduate from the Plainfield School System who has achieved some success in the world. The role model would be an important concomitant to your image as a teacher. I have reviewed your transcript and see you need one more course—'Health Education for New Jersey Teachers'—before you can be certified to teach in this state. However, we can mail this transcript to the State Department of Education and get you a temporary teaching certificate. You'll have to make up that health education course this summer."

Mr. Black made an astute observation when he first visited a classroom before starting his actual teaching job. "One thing that I observed about the students, which differed from the students of my day, was the fact that they didn't have the rigid respect, or perhaps I should say "fear," of teachers that we had. For example, the students didn't walk into the classroom and quietly take their seats. Nope! They were loud and boisterous; in fact, three of the students came into the classroom trying to mimic the "doo wop" tune of "Duke of Earl." I sat there wondering when the teacher would tell them to quiet down, but the students continued to do their thing for another five minutes. That was my first learning lesson. I realized that you can't teach in an atmosphere of noise and little discipline."

The big day arrived when Mr. Black was assigned his class. He remembered,

I was Joe Black, school teacher. As I waited for the bell to ring signaling the beginning of the school day, I wrote on the blackboard, "Mr. Black." This was to aid those students who did not remember my name. No doubt, it was a combination of my physical size and not knowing my personality that made the students file into class in an orderly manner and with a minimum of conversation. After they had all taken their seats, I smiled and said, "Good morning."

Most of the students responded with, "Good morning, Mr. Black." But one youthful male voice said, "Hi, Joe."

My education courses at Morgan State and my practice teaching experience had impressed upon me that the students would be eager to learn and would be respectful to their teachers. Although my educational preparation did not teach me how to cope with this brashness, I remained cool. While helping to integrate baseball, I learned how to smile outside and be agitated within. So I gave a little laugh and told the class to listen while I explained my identity:

"Last year I was Joe Black, baseball player, and as a fan or seeker of an autograph, you probably greeted me with 'Joe.' But now I am not a baseball player; my new profession is schoolteacher. So, respect me as a man, as an adult. As your teacher, dignity dictates that you address me as 'Mr. Black.'"

The first hurdle was cleared, easily.

You are about to find out why this chapter could too easily be called "What Goes Around Comes Around," as is the first chapter. Mr. Black and I met at Hubbard Junior High School when he was a thirty-three-year-old rookie teacher and I was a seventh grader who knew everything.

Hubbard had a diverse student population. That was one great aspect of the school. You got to know all different kinds of people. It was in a diverse town in a real melting-pot area of the state. It was a great place to learn in many different ways.

Entering Hubbard Junior High School was a little scary, even for an adolescent who "knew everything." As a seventh grader, you were bottom of the barrel. In the hallways walked huge, powerfully-built eighth and ninth graders. This was central Jersey, and a lot of these guys looked tough. I was a little shaky as I went to my first class.

I remember that Mr. Black introduced himself in that first class. He was tall, handsome, well dressed, and self-assured. He told us how fortunate we were to be at Hubbard, with our great opportunity to learn. Then he called the roll in alphabetical order. He did it with a cadence, and each student responded as he ticked off his name. He finally got to the S's: "Sanchez, Pedro, Santorini, Sal, Sears, Kenneth, Selzer, Steven."

"Here," I responded.

And then it happened. Mr. Black stopped and looked at me squarely and asked, "Are you Nathan Selzer's son?"

"Yes, sir," I replied. He stared at me, and I returned the gaze. Our eyes locked. I had never experienced anything like that before. It was electric.

From that day forth, Mr. Black was not only my teacher and baseball coach but my mentor, especially after my father passed away when I was in my twenties. And it had all begun with my father's act of kindness to a young boy, for which he needed no acknowledgment and about which he told no one. I only learned of it after my father's death from the boy, now a man, Joe Black.

As a mentor, Mr. Black emphasized the same civility that I had seen in my father. He always stressed being respectful and considerate to others. He told me that civility and professionalism went hand in hand. As a teacher, he set the civil example. In fact, when I wrote a book on civility in 2000, *By George! Mr. Washington's Guide to Civility Today*, I stated on the acknowledgments page, "Among the many teachers who played an important role in my life, none compares to Joe Black, the former Brooklyn Dodgers pitcher, who was my teacher and mentor. His counsel and civil behavior are both exemplary."[vii]

Although we never discussed the acknowledgment, Joe did tell me he was very pleased with the book and its message. It made me feel wonderful that he knew that I understood.

CHAPTER 10
Happy Hour

At Hubbard Junior High School, Mr. Black was our Health and Physical Education teacher as well as our varsity baseball coach. He infused character education into his class discussions. Mr. Black felt that behavior was a reflection of character. Our teacher wanted to build character as he taught. He believed that there must be discipline before any real teaching and learning could occur. If you acted out in his class (all male), he would invite you to Happy Hour. This was a new term for us. I found out what it meant in Mr. Black's world.

Unfortunately for me, I was one of the first to test Mr. Black. In health class, I got into a little tussle with my cousin, who had stolen my eraser. Mr. Black walked in as we were grabbing each other's arms. My cousin and I immediately received an invitation to Happy Hour. We were to report an hour before school started to the gymnasium with our gym clothes on. Mr. Black wore his P.E. sweat suit. He was imposing at six feet, two inches of muscle, with a very deep voice. For the three of us, it was a solid hour of calisthenics, with no breaks except for water. Mr. Black derived no visible pleasure from the session. He told us he wanted to impress upon us the importance of calisthenics in the care of the body. When we asked him what he meant, he asked us if we understood that our conduct had prompted him to invite us to Happy Hour. We nodded, and neither of us ever acted out or went back to Happy Hour again.

My cousin and I spread the word to our classmates about Happy Hour. Mr. Black no longer had to concern himself with the attentiveness of those pupils. His investment of one hour coming in early paid big dividends. He was willing to make the sacrifice. Discipline was established at the beginning of the semester. He was free to teach his subject without interruptions, along with lessons in character.

Years later, when I went off to college in Washington, D.C. at George Washington University, the drinking age was eighteen. Many of us had already reached that age. One day before classes started for the first semester, a bunch of us took a walk and saw a big sign on a bar near campus that said "Happy Hour—5 to 7 PM." It was exactly 5:00 p.m., and the guys all wanted to go in. I looked again at the sign and said NO. They quickly left me standing there on the sidewalk. It was one of many times I thought fondly of my teacher.

My wife and I visited a school friend named Eddie Goldstein in Colorado years later. Eddie asked me if I was still in touch with anyone at the school. When I told him I was most in touch with our old teacher, Mr. Black, he seemed surprised. Then, Eddie immediately recalled that he had acted out in class at Hubbard Junior High School and received an invitation to Happy Hour from Mr. Black. Eddie said it was one of the fairest, most enduring lessons he had ever learned. He said his respect for Mr. Black grew as a result, and he was glad to have had him as a teacher. Mr. Black was known for his fairness in all circumstances. It did not matter who or what you were—the same rules applied.

One time, one of the parents of a student who had experienced Happy Hour tested the rules, according to Joe's sister Phyllis. It turned out that Mrs. Martha Black, Joe's mother, cleaned the house of these people on a regular basis. One day, when she was doing her domestic work, the mother of the student approached Mrs. Black and asked her to tell Mr. Black not to be so hard on her son. Mrs. Black stopped the vacuum cleaner and told the woman that she did not interfere with her son and his teaching.

Whenever I encounter old junior high classmates, they always seem to name Mr. Black as the teacher they most respected. They comment that he cared about his students and encouraged their education. Many remember that he maintained a disciplined classroom but was approachable at all times to help students learn and better themselves through education. Mr. Black was always logical and reasonable. He would always call you "Mr." or "Ms.," a sign of respect he showed to all that still impresses to this day. As a teacher, he knew his subject matter thoroughly and imparted it clearly. He respected facts. Mr. Black wanted you to know what he knew so you could build on that knowledge in a meaningful way. He wanted you to learn to think in a way that made sense.

Chapter 11
Lessons Learned from Our Teacher, Mr. Black

The students at Hubbard Junior High benefitted by Mr. Black's honesty at the outset. He could have played in the major leagues for another year. Instead, he returned the contract he received over the winter from the Washington Senators with a letter to the team owner. He said that the pain in his pitching arm would not permit him to continue in professional baseball. He could have played with constant cortisone shots, or he could have played at less than his best, but he refused to do so. It would not have been right. It was a question of integrity.

Because of his strong belief in moral awareness, Mr. Black was a powerful force in educating for character. He taught his subject content well but always managed to discuss values, stressing caring, honesty, kindness, responsibility, and respect for oneself and others. Our teacher recognized that good character involved understanding, having concern for, and acting in accordance with these values, which have now been identified as the core values of character education. He not only taught us the importance of these values but he lived the values and sought to guide us in making them part of our character.

"It was our responsibility to give our best efforts to all of the students," Mr. Black said. "Our ability to make the students feel that they were 'somebody' was an important factor in attaining a high attendance and low truancy record." He believed that the difference in income levels was the 'spark' for dissension between the black and white students. "Consequently, I spent a great deal of time communicating with the students—male, female, rich, poor, black and white. I wanted to know their dreams, their hopes for the world. They didn't know in what capacity, but each of them wanted to be, or do, something that would help to make the world a better place. That was one of the things the students had in common." Regardless of your race or economic status, you could count on Mr. Black to treat you with the utmost fairness.

The words of our teacher, Mr. Black, stated over forty years ago, are still relevant in today's middle schools and high schools, "Progress, or technological advancement, helped to accentuate the differences, and this caused some attitudes of rivalry between the rich and the poor. Each of them had been content with their particular lifestyle, until the advent of television, when the impoverished were exposed constantly to the better life of their counterparts. And being human, they would sometimes fantasize that they lived in TV's make-believe world. But when they opened their front doors they faced the harsh reality of a deprived lifestyle. Imagination confronting reality often-times results in envy and/or tension. I was once in those shoes, so I could relate to their thinking that rich white people didn't think much of poor people, and I understood their bored looks when I mentioned that this was "America, land of opportunity."

Mr. Black knew that many of his students needed to learn to exercise moral reasoning. First, he thought it was necessary for each student to have good self-esteem. His mother repeatedly told him as a child, "Ain't nobody better than you, Joe." He had built on that feeling of self-worth, and he wanted it for his pupils. An example of this need for self-respect was his observation that "too often, some black students reverted to fighting to prove they were poor but they were somebody." He challenged himself to get the students to respect one another and to convince the young blacks that fisticuffs were not the way to overcome their problems. Mr. Black very clearly told us that "slinging hands" served no useful purpose. We all had talents and admirable qualities, and we should respect each other for them.

Mr. Black would tell his black students that he not only grew up poor but was often called "Old Black Joe" by schoolmates. He said that fighting didn't change anything except make your knuckles sore or loosen some teeth. Mr. Black would ask them,

"Do you want to prove that you can beat up white boys, or do you want to own a home with a lawn of green grass? Sit and think a minute; you beat up the rich kids, but you're still poor. It sounds "corny," and maybe you'll think that I'm bragging, but use me as an example. I grew up in Plainfield, was on welfare, but now I'm a teacher with a home that does not have mice or roaches. So get smart and recognize that fighting can only get you in trouble. Take advantage of this free education so you can catch up to and even pass some of these people."

There was less fighting as Mr. Black's talks gradually changed the students' attitudes. He was clearly a role model who took that position seriously and responsibly. Mr. Black would often talk about his belief that one shouldn't wait for something to happen that's going to pull you out of a situation. You get educated and compete for what's out there. So there was a great emphasis on learning and developing skills along with good character. But, there are always people who do not get it. One of them was a tall, muscular black student named Mel Ross, known throughout the school for collecting protection money every day from some of the smaller and weaker white students.

Mel Ross approached me one morning while I was changing into my street clothes after gym class in the locker room. He told me to hand over my lunch money. Talk about Murphy's Law: just at that moment, I was putting on my skivvies when Mel Ross came upon me. I did not really know what to do except to keep getting dressed. Unfortunately, my change jingled in the pocket as I put my pants on. Mel's ears perked up when he heard that sound. He held out his large hand for the money. I said no, following my father's advice.

My father had told me when I entered junior high that some guys would come around looking for my lunch money in a threatening way. He said never to pay them because you would then be paying them every day. He told me to resist, even to fight if necessary. My dad told me I might get punched or even beaten up but they would soon leave me alone in favor of easier prey. Just then, I got lucky as the bell rang and Mel left for his next class. I let out a very large sigh of relief. Saved by the bell!

Mel Ross wasn't the only one threatening the smaller guys. Central Jersey was a breeding ground for the Mafia. Some of the students in the school seemed to be training for that life. These guys were a bigger threat than Mel Ross, who was acting alone. They were more brazen and intimidating. The young leader of the future Mafia was Louis Pompano—tall, thin but muscular, with dark "Travolta" hair and very high cheekbones.

It was my misfortune that Pompano caught me after last period one day at my locker in the hallway. He demanded my money and stood in my way. When I said no, I thought he would punch me in the face. Remembering my father's words, I was prepared to stand up to him even if it meant being beaten up. But I was not going to give him any money. Instead, Louie Pompano pulled out a switchblade knife and quickly cut me on the forehead above my left eye. Blood started to gush. He must have hit a vein. I was frightened and surprised. I had never seen so much blood before. When I realized it was my blood and that Pompano cut me because he wanted my money, I felt my adrenal glands open wide. All of a sudden, I felt very strong. I punched his right hand and the knife fell. A friend of mine went running off with it. Then, I kept hitting Pompano one blow after another. I was like a mad beast. Several people had to pull me off of him, and he was actually transported to Muhlenberg Hospital. Today, I wear my scar as a badge of courage.

My father and Mr. Black both believed in standing up in that kind of situation. I was glad I had done it. It sure helped my self-respect. In no way did I gloat. I knew I had been lucky, and I was glad to still be intact. The next day, I watched my back for retaliation from one of Pompano's boys, but none came. Much later, one of his guys, John Delmonico, told me why. It was not because I was tough but because they thought I was crazy. I realized that oftentimes, when bullies are challenged or confronted, they are just not that tough. There is no real courage in being a bully.

But Louie Pompano kept up the extortion on a daily basis in the school, creating an atmosphere of fear. It was his continuing business to collect a "protection" fee from students, although the only protection it bought was for one day.   In the main hallway one day, Mr. Black approached Louie Pompano in the presence of quite a few of us. Mr. Black was wearing a tie and jacket, and at six feet, two inches, was only slightly taller than Pompano. He outweighed Pompano's 165 pounds by 50 pounds. Here is how the conversation went:

"Mr. Pompano, I want to talk to you now. You are still picking on the little white boys, and I want you to stop."

"Oh, yeah," Louie said, his voice rising.

"Mr. Pompano, you are not going to threaten those boys and take their lunch money anymore."

"I'll do what I want to do," Louie answered defiantly.

Then, Louie Pompano made the biggest mistake of his young life. He raised his right arm up in a fist, with a menacing look on his face. As soon as he did that, Mr. Black clocked him with a right to the chin. Pompano hit the floor like two sacks of potatoes.   He landed on his back with his head bouncing off the hallway floor.   It was the first time I had ever seen smelling salts fail to revive someone. Louie Pompano was taken to the hospital.   There he was treated, quickly recovered, and was in school the next day, but his "protection" business was at an end.

That was probably the only way at that point in time to stop this practice that had always existed in the school.   Mr. Black had ended the extortion racket in the school in the only way possible despite his beliefs about violence.   He had to know he was putting his job at risk but he saw no alternative.

Of course, now the big concern was for Mr. Black's job. Our most respected teacher had laid hands on a student, something that was strictly forbidden. He had been courageously looking out for us. A meeting was set up with the Superintendent of Schools, a white-haired gentleman who was very conservative. We all crowded into the auditorium in City Hall on Watchung Avenue for the hearing. It was standing room only. Here is what went on after the meeting was called to order:

Superintendent Podesta: Mr. Black, we were very glad that you decided to teach in the Plainfield School System when you left professional baseball. You have earned respect as a dedicated educator in the short time you have been at Hubbard Junior High School.

Mr. Black (wearing a suit and tie): Thank you, sir. I find my job very rewarding.

Superintendent Podesta: But the problem we have now is a major one, Mr. Black. It is very serious. A teacher cannot hit a boy.

Mr. Black (looking the Superintendent in the eye while speaking slowly in his deep voice): Sir, you are a boy until you raise up (gesturing with his right arm lifted and raised in a fist), and then you become a man.

The place broke out in applause. We students were up on our feet, wildly cheering and applauding. We had never heard such an explanation. So few words. Such good reasoning. So cool.

The Superintendent took it all in and reacted by immediately dismissing the charges and adjourning the meeting. Mr. Black was still going to be with us at school. This was fairness and justice in action.

Chapter 12
The Difference between Wrestling and "Rasslin"

Mr. Black felt that wrestling would be a healthy form of exercise, involving discipline and knowledge as well as brawn. It would also serve to improve the relationships between what he called the "have's" and the "have-nots." The tough guys would gain a new appreciation for the agility, coordination, and balance of their smaller peers.

The first match involved a 120-pound eighth grader and Mr. Black. Everyone laughed at the prospect until the student quickly grabbed the teacher's right arm, turned, and flipped Mr. Black over his shoulder on to the mat. There was a loud bam. The observers went "ooh" and "aah." All were impressed. Even the rough and tough were amazed at what know-how could do.

Then, Mr. Black brought in Mr. John Pepe, an intercollegiate wrestling champion at Penn State and now varsity wrestling coach at Plainfield High, to teach us the basic skills. Although he was a small, wiry man, Mr. Pepe used his knowledge and agility to throw Mr. Black, reinforcing the earlier lesson. Mr. Pepe remained to teach us the rules of wrestling, showing us why each rule made sense. After Mr. Pepe finished, Mr. Black pointed out that in wrestling, there are rules, not like in "rasslin." He emphasized that rules must always be respected since they ensured equal treatment for everyone. Mr. Black said that was true in life as well as in wrestling and other sports.

Mr. Black then had us square off for individual matches based on our size. Unfortunately for me, he set me up to wrestle a guy known for his toughness, John Centorini. It was his idea of having a "have" and a "have-not" square off for all to see. We wrestled using all the skills we could summon. John was strong and I could not defeat him. I was quick and he could not defeat me. We were both spent after a few minutes. Mr. Black commented, "Both of these youngsters proved that they were champions because, at the conclusion of their two-round match, the new respect and admiration that they had for one another was more important than who won." From that day forward, John Centorini and I always acknowledged each other in the hallway when we passed.

Here is what Mr. Black had to say after reflecting about this activity. "The positive showings in our combative classes gave the rich kids the courage not to give in when asked to pay protection money. And soon the after-school fighting and coercion became a thing of the past. The body slams to the mat accelerated the day, creating greater unity and understanding among the students of Hubbard Junior High School." He reiterated that all must learn to respect rules.

Mr. Black saw respect as a key, vital value. He believed what author Patricia McGerr wrote in her short story *Johnny Lingo's Eight-Cow Wife*: "Every human being from cradle to coffin responds to people who see and draw out their hidden potential. You see it in their countenance; you hear it in their voice. No, they may not all turn into physical beauties, but their inner beauty will shine in ways that I believe will significantly influence their physical presence and bring new light to their eyes." Mr. Black viewed respect as a cornerstone in character development. He especially understood and appreciated the following idea, which Ms. McGerr went on to observe in her story: "Some people are born into environments where there is no respect, and often their behavior and personality reflect the void. But sometimes it only takes one person giving them respect to change everything."

It is too bad Aretha Franklin did not record her smash hit "Respect" until a few years later, in 1967, because it would have been Mr. Black's anthem with his students. He strongly believed that you earn respect, give respect, get respect, and always show respect under normal circumstances. He encouraged respect for others and for life itself. He himself commanded respect with his caring, other-directed attitude. It was important to him that his students respect their educations and build on their self-respect to live positive, civil, and productive lives.

Mr. Joe Black wanted for his students what Stephen Covey, in his book, *Everyday Greatness*, called "primary greatness," which includes "character and contribution, as distinguished from 'secondary greatness,' which has to do with notoriety, wealth, fame, prestige, or position."[viii] Martha Jo Black, Joe's daughter, mentioned in her introduction to this book that Joe taught her the importance of this difference.

Chapter 13
Teaching Teenagers How to Manage Anger

Mr. Black dealt primarily with adolescent boys who were growing up in a tough town and felt a lot of frustration in their lives. Teenagers are famous for immaturity and lack of good judgment. In the town there was a great disparity in wealth, with neighborhoods both affluent and poor. There was also a mix of many different cultures, with a sizable minority population, mostly black. There was extortion. There was dissing. There was fighting.

By fostering an atmosphere of fairness, safety, and respect, Mr. Black hoped to improve the environment for learning and personal development. The Louie Pompano incident was a matter of safety. It was an exercise in self-defense, and it broke up a practice that caused great daily anxiety among the students. What he did greatly improved an ongoing, threatening situation. Mr. Black was tremendously respected for his courageous action, which put his very job at risk.

Mr. Black knew that disrespect was the root of a lot of negative activity. He tried to foster mutual respect between students, as he did with Joe Centorini and me. He always showed respect for all students. He believed that a show of disrespect led immediately to anger. Mr.

Black was an early promoter of what we now call "anger management." He believed the adage "If you are patient in one moment of anger, you will escape a hundred days of sorrow."

Mr. Black promoted the idea that all people deserve respect simply because they are human beings. He made certain that no one stepped on the dignity of another. Since he knew that anger was a destructive force and would occur despite our efforts to prevent it, he taught us how to deal with it.

Mr. Black taught anger control in his usual practical way. He would tell us, "Smart fish don't bite. They do not take the bait. Anger is the result of your thoughts in reaction to someone's words or actions." When people said and did things to get our goat, he would encourage us to laugh it off.

Our wise teacher told us that everyone, including him, gets invited to "anger parties." The key is not to accept the invitations. We must never respond to anger with anger. That is how things escalate. He would have us all take a deep breath before we calmly responded, if a response was necessary. He expressed the thought that anger can be managed if you do not react to the feeling.

One day in his classroom, Mr. Black hung up two large photographs. One of the photos was of the door to the principal's office, and the other was of the vice principal's office. His point was that you should pause to consider the potential consequences of acting out on anger. We all knew that our parents would be contacted by the principal or vice principal if we got in trouble. If we were suspended, our parents would have to accompany us to the principal's office to have the suspension terminated. It was the old idea of thinking before acting, and anticipating the consequences of your actions.

Chapter 14
Teaching Us the Old Native American Prayer

Mr. Black taught us a great lesson about anger, misunderstanding, and conflict one day at an assembly of the whole school. School administration felt that discipline had to be in place before there could be meaningful education. With this in mind, they asked our most respected teacher to give a short talk.

First, Mr. Black discussed the problem of acting out when angry. He stated that these harmful reactions could be short-circuited. Dealing with anger, he said, includes avoiding snap judgments; if you can try to imagine being in the other person's shoes, your perspective changes.

This man of stature then stepped to the front of the stage and away from the microphone. In his deep, strong voice, he told us, "There is an old Native American prayer: 'Oh Great Spirit, grant me the wisdom to walk in another's moccasins before I criticize or pass judgment.' Mr. Black believed it was important to our character to develop empathy skills. He thought we would treat others in a more kind, considerate, understanding, and respectful way if we worked on obtaining a highly developed sense of empathy. He was able to tell the tough kids that he "lived where they did, in the shanties by the track." He advised, "Sting a young man's conscience and reward him with a little honest hope."

For the first time, many of us were struck with the notion that everyone comes from a different place and may not realize due to their circumstances that they are causing others to feel anger. On the other hand, they might just be on overload and not feeling good. So, why take the bait when we can simply move on?

Mr. Black gave us some new insights at a relatively young age. It has become clear to me that he believed civil behavior was not only the right way to act, but life's lubricant. Our teacher not only created an environment where greater empathy and caring resulted in less conflict, but he helped to create a sense of community within our school. His inspirational stories, his exemplary and courageous behavior, and his caring and concerned dedication to our education and character made a powerful impact. Many lives were affected for the better. This is the kind of influence a great character education teacher can have. This is the reason why teachers should not only be respected but revered if they are sincere educators concerned about both our academic and character development. In Mr. Black's case, fairness to all was his overriding concern.

He understood fairness to mean that we are all connected as people and should be treated equally. We are all part of the school and the community. That means no one should be left out or alienated. All must be recognized in this patchwork fabric of humanity. Being part of that quilt is what moves us collectively in a supportive and positive direction.

Chapter 15
A Major Leaguer as Junior High Baseball Coach

Of course we were thrilled to have Mr. Black, a former major league pitcher, as our baseball coach. Our Dodger-style practice drills left us with a great sense of pride in ourselves and our team. He taught us the fundamental skills of baseball. Interdependence was an important theme in his teaching—we were all important parts of the whole, and the whole was always greater than the sum of its parts.

Coach Black would not allow his pitchers to throw curveballs. He believed pitching a baseball was an unnatural action and that throwing "breaking" pitches placed an additional strain on the muscles and bones. This was particularly so with youthful arms, which were not fully developed. All the pitchers wanted to throw curves but he would not permit it. Instead, he emphasized control. Coach would rather lose a game than cause one of his pitchers to have arm trouble.

A bunch of us on the team thought we could really hit the ball. As adolescent males, we were cocky; we thought we were invincible. We could hit any pitcher including the coach. At one practice, we urged him to get on the mound and give us his best stuff. He did that day, and Harvey Fisher, our slugging catcher, goaded me to get up to the plate. He yelled out, "Selzer, he's all washed up. He's got nothing left. The majors are history. Whack it!" The other guys jumped in to incite me to face Coach Black.

Now, I was a decent *junior high school* hitter. In my pubescent ignorance and due to the spirited urging of my teammates, I picked up a bat and dug in at the plate. I really thought I could hit the big guy. A sheepish grin crossed the coach's face as he set to pitch. What we had was a right-handed pitcher against a slight but confident right-handed batter. Coach wound up and threw a pitch. I had never seen a ball move so fast. I thought it would hit me on the back and I went down. Instead, the ball curved five feet to the left to hit the outside corner—a strike. As I wiped the dirt from my uniform and the humiliation from my face, I realized that I had never seen a major league curveball before. From the hush of my mates, they had not either. Our big mouths were silenced. It was really something to see. Coach could not hide his smile at our reactions. He said nothing. How lucky were we to have Mr. Black as our teacher and coach.

During the season the coach worked patiently with us to teach us the game he loved. He would encourage us to improve on our weaknesses, which were many. He taught us the importance of following his signals from the coaching box. He made smart runners out of all of us. Coach Black taught us the mental side of baseball as well as the physical. He stressed teamwork and gave even the weaker players a chance to play. All they had to do was play hard. Coach Black admired "heart" in players such as Bobby Duchin, only five feet, four inches tall. He wrote that "desire, dedication, and guts are the elements that Bobby gave to our team." Bobby played like he was an All-Star after Coach Black praised him for these qualities. It was a vivid example of how attitude affects ability.

Coach Joe Black tried to make teamwork, fair play, and sportsmanship the most important parts of playing baseball on our team. The following story demonstrates the values he tried to instill:

One of our players was attempting to "stretch" a single into a double; when he realized he was not going to make it, he attempted to knock the ball out of the hands of the defending player. However, instead of a hard slide, he leaped, spikes first, into the chest of the second baseman. I commended the effort but I did not condone unsportsmanlike conduct. I reprimanded my player and told him to go over and apologize to the injured player. He gave me a look of arrogance and announced, "I ain't gonna apologize to nobody."

I explained to him that baseball was a game and no man is bigger than the game. So, he was out of the game and off the team. My actions surprised the other players because the dismissed player was one of my better hitters. But it made them realize that I was serious when I stated that we would play hard, but fair.

There was another benefit being on Coach Black's baseball team. Each spring he took us to Yankee Stadium for a game. We got there early, and he took us down near the field. Then he would say, "Hey, Mickey, come on over and meet my team."

Ole' Number 7 Mickey Mantle would reply, "Sure, Joe. How are you doing?"

We were awestruck as photos were taken, to be cherished forever. When my two sons were younger and collecting baseball cards, I found the picture in a desk drawer and proudly pulled it out. "What do you guys think of this?" They looked at the old black and white photo.

Their eyes got bigger when they saw Number 7 in pinstripes. Then, they replied in unison, "It would be good if you weren't in it, Dad."

It was at one of these games at Yankee Stadium that Mr. Black encountered author Roger Kahn, who later wrote the classic book about the old Dodgers. They knew each other from Kahn's days as a newspaper and magazine sports reporter.

Kahn asked, "What are you doing now, Joe?"

Joe replied, "Getting my Master's at Seton Hall. I'm back in Plainfield, New Jersey, where I started teaching and coaching at the junior high school. This is my team. I've come to introduce them to the manager."

Legendary Yankee manager Casey Stengel was leaning on the batting cage, watching Yogi Berra, Mickey Mantle, and Roger Maris take their strokes.

"Hey, Skip," Mr. Black called. "You got a minute?"

Stengel turned and approached. "Yes, sir, yes, sir. I remember ya. Good fast one. What's all that ya got behind ya there?"

Coach said, "This is my team, Case. They're having troubles. They've lost sixteen out of eighteen games, and I wondered what the old master thought I ought to teach 'em."

"Lost sixteen of eighteen, you say?" Casey Stengel scratched his chin. "Well, first you better teach 'em to lose in the right spirit."

Just as Joe had benefitted from the knowledge and guidance of Roy Campanella, Joe had his players learn from Campy. A serious automobile accident had left Campanella in a wheelchair but Joe still "leaned" on him. Joe explained: "On several occasions the catchers from my junior high school baseball team and I would drive to New York so that Campanella could teach them the mechanics of catching. If his accident left him with feelings of self-pity, I was never exposed to that Campanella. It was a thrill to sit there and listen to Campy glorify the position of catcher. As the old-timers used to say, Campy was a real 'gamer.'"

Chapter 16
The End of Joe's Formal Teaching Career

The Plainfield School System had the benefit of Mr. Black as a teacher for seven years. He viewed it as a meaningful career. He said it helped him to grow as a person. The students made him feel as though he was needed, he said with humility. It was satisfying for him to think that he had made a positive contribution to their growth and development. He hoped he had contributed to the character development of his students. Mr. Black did this by showing respect to his students and teaching and reinforcing important values. Is it any wonder the respect was returned?

Here is a clear illustration of the respect he received as a teacher. A student stole a watch from Mr. Black's desk. The next day he returned the watch to Mr. Black. When Mr. Black asked why, he explained that some of the guys had threatened to beat him up if he didn't give it back.

Another example occurred after a policeman in town was grazed with a bullet. The police suspected a Hubbard student so they asked Mr. Black if he would help them get the gun. Mr. Black promised to help as long as he did not have to provide names. Then, in each class, he discussed the incident and explained that he didn't want names; he just wanted the gun in the bottom drawer of his desk. At 3:00 p.m., as he was preparing to go home, Mr. Black opened the bottom drawer and the gun was there.

The final assembly in 1963 gave both the students and Mr. Black an opportunity to say good-bye. Mr. Black had a family to support and—as unfortunately is often the case today—he could not afford to continue teaching. The guys on the baseball team at the time had pooled their limited resources and presented Mr. Black with an attaché case and pen and pencil set for his new career with Greyhound Corporation. He acknowledged this sincere gesture with a lump in his throat.

At that final assembly, Mr. Black made a present to the school as well. He presented a framed copy of "A Game Guy's Prayer" to Hubbard Junior High. It was to be hung in the front hall to be read by any student experiencing feelings of hopelessness. It had been read on a national television show by famed Yankees announcer Mel Allen as a tribute to Roy Campanella, the great Dodger catcher paralyzed in an auto accident. Talk about courage—Roy Campanella's autobiography is titled *It's Good to be Alive.*[ix]

A Game Guy's Prayer

Help me to be a sport in this little game of life. I don't ask for any place in the line up; play me where you need me. I only ask for the stuff to give you a hundred percent of what I've got. If all the hard drives come my way, I thank you for the compliment. Help me to remember you won't let anything come that you and I together can't handle. And help me to take the bad breaks as part of the game. Help make me thankful for them.

And, God, help me to always play on the square no matter what the other players do. Help me to come clean. Help me to see that often the best part of the game is helping other guys. Help me to be a "regular fellow" with the other players.

Finally, God, if fate seems to uppercut me with both hands and I am laid up on the shelf in sickness or old age, help me to take that as a part of the game also. Help me not to whimper or squeal that the game was a frame-up or that I had a raw deal. When in the dusk I get the final bell, I ask for no lying, complimentary stones. I'd only like to know that you feel I've been a good guy.

Author unknown

Chapter 17
The Greyhound Years

It was a shame that Mr. Black could not make enough money in teaching and coaching to take care of his family. He even worked part time at a department store. While he was teaching, he had studied at night at both Rutgers and Seton Hall universities to receive a Master's degree to add to his BA from Morgan State College (now University). He was so intellectually curious that in his late sixties, he was admitted to and attended law school at Arizona State University. He told me he enjoyed arguing points of the law in class with the young ones. Joe was amused and amazed at their naiveté. He laughingly noted that they sometimes forgot that common sense and practical thinking were important as well as legal theory. He was a great asset to the vital classroom discussions. Mr. Black not only preached education, but he practiced what he preached. He loved learning all of his life.

His educational background and substance of character attracted the executives at the Greyhound Corporation. He had made it clear that he would not be a "token" to be showcased. He was assured he would occupy a meaningful position with Greyhound Lines in 1963. Former Chairman and CEO John Teets said he always included Joe Black in his senior-level meetings, although he did not have to do so. It was important to him that Joe be kept abreast of all corporate affairs. He noted that Joe Black was not only intelligent, but he possessed a great deal of common sense, which benefitted the company. He contributed in a positive way at these meetings. Mr. Joe Black had made it clear that he would learn the transportation industry and be a responsible member of the corporate team. Greyhound executive Joe Black would work hard in Chicago and then in Phoenix (when the company relocated in 1971) to establish his credibility in the business world.

When Joe first arrived in Chicago with the Greyhound job, Mr. John H. Johnson, president of Johnson Publishing Company, met with him. Mr. Johnson, the very successful publisher of *Ebony* and *Jet* magazines, befriended Joe and asked him over lunch whether he had resigned his teaching position. When Joe informed him that he had not, Mr. Johnson suggested that Joe should "seek a leave of absence rather than resign because some of the jobs [were] being created from the hysteria of the civil rights movement."

Mr. Johnson further said that Joe should allow himself time to determine whether the Greyhound position was a real job. "And to magnify his suggestion," Joe explained, "he went into his wallet and gave me a folded, well-worn paper to read. It was a leave of absence from the U.S. Post Office. He explained that when he decided to publish his magazine he wasn't quite certain that his self-confidence and a dream assured success so he wanted to protect his family from the agonies of him being an unemployed 'breadwinner.'"

"Needless to say, I heeded his advice." When Joe spoke to Dr. Podesta, Plainfield's Superintendent of Schools, Dr. Podesta said, "Joe, if you return to the teaching profession, we want you to do it in Plainfield, so we will give you a three-year leave of absence. In that time you'll know if the Greyhound offer is a real opportunity or a show." Dr. Podesta's offer showed great understanding for the situation and respect for Joe as a teacher.

The Greyhound job turned out to be a substantial opportunity with real growth potential. Joe started his career in 1962 as a New York-based Special Markets Representative for Greyhound Lines, Inc. He was promoted to Chicago and the national marketing staff as Director of Markets in 1963. In that position he caused Greyhound to gain favorable publicity through the years because he instituted Special Markets' Woman of the Year Luncheons, Father of the Year Luncheons, Senior Citizens Information Luncheons, Career Opportunity Luncheons, and Drug/Alcohol Abuse Seminars.

The success of these community relations endeavors earned Joe Black the promotion to Vice President - Special Markets for Greyhound Lines, Inc. In 1967 this advancement gave Joe Black the distinction of being the first black vice president of a major transportation company.

Joe Black continued to move forward and in 1969 he was made an officer of The Greyhound Corporation, one of Fortune's top 500 companies. This was the parent company. In his role as Vice President - Special Markets for The Greyhound Corporation, Joe Black encouraged the hiring and training of "hard core" applicants; upward mobility for minority group workers within the corporate family; utilization of minority group advertising outlets; placing of funds in minority group banks; purchasing goods or services from minority vendors; and setting up an extensive scholarship program.

Joe Black's career with Greyhound lasted twenty-five years. He started at ground level and worked his way up in making the transition from educator to business executive. In his job, he was able to assist others in their educational goals by setting up a scholarship program. There are many people out there who owe him a great debt of gratitude. By 1983, the Greyhound annual scholarship program generated $130,000, distributed among forty-two colleges and universities. This sum did not include the Greyhound contribution to the United Negro College Fund.

According to Mr. Teets, Joe Black also brought much goodwill to Greyhound Corporation. He gave many talks at schools of all levels about the importance of education and of working hard at school and on the job. He initiated drug and alcohol abuse seminars. His people skills, coupled with his intelligence and positive demeanor, were a great asset to the company. He appeared on many television shows, such as the Today show with Joe Garagiola, giving Greyhound what he called "favorable identification."

After formally retiring from the company in 1987, Joe continued to provide valuable service and counsel to Viad Corporation (formerly Greyhound and Dial Corporations) as a consultant. He also served as a consultant to the Commissioner of Baseball.

Joe was recruited by Jerry Colangelo of the Arizona Diamondbacks, which began operations in 1998. Joe was asked to assist with baseball and community endeavors to introduce professional baseball to Arizona. Jerry Colangelo, chairman of the team, said that Joe educated him well and thoroughly. He appointed Joe an ambassador for the team. Up until that time, Colangelo had owned the Chicago Bulls and later the Phoenix Suns. His knowledge was in professional basketball. He credits Joe Black's "reservoir of information" and "passion for the game" with helping him put together a successful new baseball organization.

The "Arizona Diamondbacks 2002 Community Report" says that, "With Joe, the Arizona Diamondbacks' Community Affairs department boasted an unbeatable combination of baseball tradition, business experience, and Arizona knowledge." It went on to say, "As a community relations representative, Joe spent much of his time conducting outreach to Arizona communities. He was instrumental in developing the Arizona Diamondbacks' speakers bureau and spent much of his time speaking to groups and educating them about baseball and its rich tradition. Joe Black was extremely powerful at delivering and describing baseball's meaning to a person and to a community." There is a large, tasteful image of a baseball with the words "Joe Black 1924-2002" on it in the outfield of the stadium. Martha Jo Black and Chico Black were there at the dedication.

Chapter 18
"By The Way"

During the Greyhound years, Joe Black had an opportunity to provide commentary for a syndicated newspaper and magazines (*Jet* and *Ebony*) column called "By the Way." There were numerous spots on radio. A friend of mine, George Simms, attorney at law, grew up in the District of Columbia. When he was in high school, he woke up to "By the Way" with Joe Black on the WOL radio station every school day. George said the messages were always inspirational, especially coming from a vice president of Greyhound Corporation. He told me he did not even know that Joe Black had been a major leaguer until he visited his aunt, who subscribed to *Jet*. He picked up her magazine and read about Joe Black's sports past which preceded a syndicated "By the Way" column in the magazine. George Simms is now a respected team leader as an Assistant State's Attorney for Montgomery County, Maryland. He feels a debt of gratitude to Joe Black for the inspirational, motivational, thoughtful comments.

According to Joe, the idea of the "By the Way" commentaries was to provoke thought. They appeared from 1969 through 1980 in the aforementioned magazines and in forty newspapers. He was both applauded and cursed for his commentary but the majority of the response was positive. What was supposed to be a one-year venture went on for twelve years and reached millions of people.

In one of the columns, he explained the purpose of his writing:

"BY THE WAY"

For many of you, I'd like to take a minute and tell you what Joe Black is all about.

What I'm about is an examination of the problems all blacks share—not the expression of one man's interest, ego, or experience but rather the contributions of many people and much common sense. I am merely the catalyst. You see, I do not believe we must foster hate and violence to keep moving forward, although I understand as well as anyone why many think we should. I've been there and endured the harassment, ridicule, and rudeness, back when we were integrating the Big Leagues. But, I also found myself in a comfortable enough position to wonder what all the shouting, singing, marching, and boycotts were all about when the Movement began to gain momentum. Except for supporting memberships in the NAACP and Urban League, I accepted the rewards of the Movement passively, which wasn't exactly paying one's dues.

Then I met Dr. Martin Luther King, Jr. and learned the many ways a black can aid the cause, and how much greater the Movement is than the individual. At that time, too, my mother died, a lady who spent a lifetime keeping a family together while finding time to do for others. That combination of circumstances taught me to extend my hand, to help black people understand our responsibilities, within our community, during our quest for equality of opportunity—and to help de-emphasize hate.

That, and simply that, is what Joe Black and By-the-Way are all about. The man was clothed in principled honesty. If that is a redundancy, so be it. His words would ring true. When intelligence, reason, sincerity, and frankness combine with empirical knowledge, what you have is the real thing. There is no substitute for that kind of genuineness and pragmatic truth.

Below is a sample commentary from "By the Way" on a topic Joe often spoke to us about in school:

"BY THE WAY"

Ever since I was a small boy, the word "quitter" had a bad meaning. Calling another kid a quitter was a sure invitation to a rap in the mouth. Today, there's a new word that means almost the same thing as "quitter." That word is "drop-out." It's used to describe thousands of young Americans who just up and quit when the going gets rough at school or on a job.

Of course, quitting is a cinch! You just walk away! And for the time being, you're the boss. Your own man. Free as a bird. And you've got something going for you. You're young. And because you're young, people excuse a lot of things. You don't beat up a baby for breaking his bottle. But old father time soon comes along swinging his scythe. You get older. People stop feeling sorry for you, stop trying to understand you. And then it hits you. You're uneducated. Trained for nothing but being angry.

Sad picture? You bet! Because what you don't do for yourself when you're young, in the way of training and learning and education, you just can't make up in that short time ahead, when you're older.

Sound like corn? Most real-life things do. But while you've got your youth, you can turn things around. But you've gotta have guts. Because it's a lot tougher to drop IN than it was to drop out. Think about that and remember what that old philosopher known as "Anonymous" once said. "Grab onto life when you're young, 'cause you're not going to pass this way again."

Joe Black's words of wisdom were appreciated by many. His column and radio spots were very popular. There were certain recurring themes that he emphasized even when he had spoken to us as students. One of these themes was the subject of the following column.

"BY THE WAY"

There's an important fourteen letter word in our language today that many of us tend to overlook. A word some of us even seem to forget. The word isn't necessarily black jargon. Nor, even exclusively created for black usage. But it is a word that applies to us all. And one we should never forget.

What's the word? Responsibility. Your and my responsibility to today's and tomorrow's society. During the trials and troubles of today, too often many of us sit back and let someone else do all our talking for us. (It's understandable why.) But too often the people who we let talk are merely seeking popularity through the manipulations of emotions. People who spend all their time shouting racism and hatred. You know them. Sure you do. People who, in the long run, could be leading us all down the road to nowhere. And, incidentally, perhaps getting a little rich along the way, too. I don't know about you but I for one am mighty tired of living in a society that, instead of being filled with love, and brotherhood and cool heads, and understanding, seems more abundant in hate, and tension, and greed, and jealousy.

What can we do? Well, that's where the word "responsibility" comes in. As Malcolm X once said, "If you don't think for yourself, if you don't see for yourself, then you will end up hating your friends, and loving your enemies."

Do you want to be responsible for something like that happening? I doubt it. But the question then remains: do you want to be responsible for something better happening? I think we all do.

"BY THE WAY"

"Be honest with everyone ... especially yourself." That's a little saying I heard a long time ago. It's not very eloquent or clever, but I like it. It sums up in a phrase, the essence of a series of Greyhound Community Service ads entitled: By The Way, by Joe Black.

The ads are placed in black newspapers. Adaptations of them are heard over black-oriented radio stations. They are written in an effort to shake people out of their complacency about subjects of great concern to the black community. In these ads, I say what I believe ... not necessarily what I think you want to hear.

So, when you hear my voice on the air, or read my words in the paper, remember that they are not merely to inform or impose my views upon you ... but simply to make you think about things in a way you may not have thought about them before.

I am not a preacher or a teacher. I'm citizen Joe Black, fortunate enough to be able to talk to thousands of people and hopefully influence them to re-examine solutions to black problems in a new and constructive light. I still feel strongly that the things that unite people of good will are much more important than the things that divide them.

"By The Way," by Joe Black, is just one small voice asking humbly for a little more sanity, a little more honesty, and a lot more thinking through of what we are doing and the methods we are using to realistically solve the problems of our black community.

"BY THE WAY"

Lately it seems that many of the anchors that people depended upon to steady themselves during periods of trial have gone down the drain. Faith in God, faith in people, faith in yourself, and faith in the future suddenly seem to be running second to a fist in the mouth, dissension, anger, violence, sit-ins, strikes, and riots. I'm not so naive to think that a few well chosen words from me are going to change all that. But I do believe that somebody's got to start somewhere. That's why I make it my business to visit schools and places where young people gather. When I talk with them, I try to leave them with a creed. It's not very profound. But it touches on some things that are basic and real. It goes like this:

Lord, teach me that sixty seconds make a minute, sixteen ounces a pound, and one hundred cents a dollar. Help me to lie down at night with a clear conscience, unhaunted by faces of those to whom I may have brought pain. Grant that I may earn my meal ticket on the square and in earning it may do unto others as I would have them do unto me. Blind me to the faults of other fellows and reveal to me my own. Help me to be young enough to laugh with children, yet mature enough to be considerate of old age.

And when comes the day of darkening shades, make the ceremony short, make the epitaph simple ... "Here lies a man."

"BY THE WAY"

For those who think that school is a "waste," listen as Elmon Prier describes a dropout.

D -   Destruction of the mind's ability to grow; defeat by the school system in reaching you; defeat of your parents' desires to see you succeed.

R -   Running away from responsiblity of becoming an educated person; refusing to cope; retreating from reality; running on empty.

O -   Operating your life without regard for the future.

P -   Preparing yourself for guaranteed failure.

O -   Opting to survive without a diploma (fat chance!); opting for ignorance.

U -   Unemployment awaits you because you are unprepared, uneducated, unskilled, under-employed, and unwanted.

T -   Tuning out the world that has not reached you; turning to alternatives that usually spell troubles, trials, and tribulations.

That spells dropout!

"BY THE WAY"

A group of famous people in the entertainment world came together and blended their voices in song and said:

"We are the world
We are the children
We are the ones to make a brighter day."

This unselfish act was motivated by the famine and starvation in Ethiopia. It is a classic example of "black and white together, we shall overcome."

Today, I want to remind you of a challenge to black Americans. It is finding a cure for Sickle Cell Trait and Sickle Cell Anemia. Why? Because one of 12 black Americans has Sickle Cell Trait; one of 500 black Americans has Sickle Cell Anemia. Sickle Cell Anemia does not affect one's intelligence, but it can cause growth retardation, leg ulcers, pneumonia, strokes, decreased exercise tolerance, and sometimes cause pain.

If you are born with this tendency from one parent, you have Sickle Cell Trait. If you are born with this tendency from both parents, you have Sickle Cell Anemia. You will not know whether you have Sickle Cell Trait unless you take a simple blood test. So help combat and support the fight against Sickle Cell Disease by:

1. Having a blood test to learn if you have the Trait.

2. Riding Greyhound, because in 1986 a percentage of each ticket will be donated to the National Association for Sickle Cell Disease.

3. Mailing a contribution to your local Sickle Cell Disease Chapter, or to:

The National Association for Sickle Cell Disease
4221 Wilshire Boulevard
Los Angeles, California 90010-3503

"BY THE WAY"

Sometimes the criticism that I receive because of my "By The Way" commentaries makes me 'Feel Like A Motherless Child', alone and misunderstood. And there have been moments when those feelings made me pause and wonder why I should continue to put myself in the position of being castigated.

That's when I remind myself that I was not seeking popularity, no, it was my intent to encourage people to strive for success by utilizing the minds and bodies given to us by God. So here I go again with another commentary.

Black athletes are now challenged to be achieving students as well as performers in the sports arena. The NCAA has ruled that starting with September 1986, all incoming freshman must have a 2.0 scholastic average or score a minimum of 700 on the S.A.T. exams. This is not a racist move; it is an attempt to remind the athletes that they are students, not balls.

Excelling in the classroom will not diminish the athlete's ability to perform on the athletic field. The athletes who are successful as students are a definite asset to black America. You see, black people don't need more athletic heros, but we do need more doctors, lawyers, teachers, and engineers.

Mr. Black as our teacher would constantly and gently remind us that being responsible means doing the things you say you will do. It is being dependable and accountable. Anyone, Joe would say, who valued friendships or personal and professional relationships needed to show responsibility. He further explained that being responsible was being trustworthy and being someone who kept promises. Mr. Black noted often that being responsible earns you respect and even admiration. He mixed teaching academics with stressing the importance of respect and responsibility. This is why I believe he was a true character educator.

In his travels for Greyhound, Vice President Black would have the opportunity to meet many prominent people from the worlds of business, politics, entertainment, and high education. One time he spotted Dr. Martin Luther King Jr. in Newark (N.J.) Airport while preparing to return to Chicago. He approached Dr. King to extend greetings and renewed their relationship. They each had some time before their flights so Mr. Black asked Dr. King why the movement was non-violent.

Dr. King explained, "You see, others can rationalize their use of force if we become violent by projecting the 'eye for an eye' theory. But it is difficult for them to justify hurting people just because they are marching and chanting slogans or singing songs about rights and freedom granted to citizens of this country."

Mr. Black thanked him and vowed to himself that he would have a greater involvement. And he did. In 1987, Mrs. Coretta Scott King selected Joe Black to receive the Martin Luther King Distinguished Service Award, which he treasured.

Another recurring theme of Joe Black's persona was his view of the importance of the quality of respect. In a "By the Way" column he said, "Respect isn't easy to earn. It takes time. Patience. And perhaps most important, it takes working at. The man who earns the respect of his family will be, truly, a family leader. And it won't be because of what he says. But rather, what he does. And how well he does it. And how consistently. A man stands as tall as the things he does."

The column clearly encouraged people to improve themselves and society in general. And it has stood the test of time.

Chapter 19
Staying in Touch with His Students

My relationship to Joe was always meaningful to me. Here was this busy man who still had time to devote to his former students. Throughout the years, he told me what other former classmates were doing as well. He was especially proud of those who were helping others. Mr. Black was never too busy to help guide us. He took a particular interest in those of us who played baseball on his school team because he knew us best. He wanted to see us have successful careers.

One of the guys on our baseball team (to my right in the team photo from 1961) was Vic Washington. Vic was a great athlete who excelled in all sports that he attempted. At Plainfield High School, he was a star in baseball, football, and track. On the football team, Vic was a running back who averaged ten yards a carry. He was just about an automatic first down every time he touched the ball.

Mr. Black had hoped that Vic Washington would pursue a Major League Baseball career but Vic opted for football. Nevertheless, Mr. Black helped Vic obtain a football scholarship to the University of Wyoming, where he made All-American. When Vic ran into some difficulties at school, Mr. Black was there for him. Vic trusted Mr. Black from the days when Mr. Black dealt with his issues in junior high school. Mr. Black stayed in touch with Vic during his career in professional football in Canada, followed by nine years as a receiver and punt returner in the National Football League. After that, Mr. Black continued to maintain contact to see how he could help Vic in business.

Another student that Mr. Black enjoyed being in touch with was Bruce Levine. Bruce had been a catcher on our baseball team and was a real field general. Mr. Black nurtured that leadership quality by playing him slightly more than a younger black catcher who was technically better but less confident on the ballfield. Coach Black felt the younger player would have his turn. Race was not a factor. Bruce appreciated Coach Black's fairness. Mr. Black was pleased that his field general went on after college to have a very successful business career. Bruce would maintain contact by participating in fundraising events put on by BAT, the Baseball Assistance Team, a non-profit organization founded by Joe in 1986—one near and dear to his heart.

Chapter 20
BAT

The purpose of the Baseball Assistance Team (BAT) is to assist former major league ballplayers who did not play long enough to qualify for a pension or who have fallen on hard times. BAT recognizes that the lives of baseball players continue after their active careers end. For some, especially those who played before the days of escalating salaries and generous pension plans, circumstances can become difficult. BAT provides health care, financial grants, and rehabilitative counseling (whatever form is required) to attain a level of comfort and dignity for former players and their families with demonstrated needs. It now has an office in New York in the same suite occupied by Major League Baseball. With his charitable nature, Joe Black was very involved with BAT, as was his dear friend, Joe Garagiola, the big-hearted former catcher and Sportscasters Hall of Fame member. Joe Black held the title of vice president. They were both on the BAT Grant Committee at the same time.

After being formed in 1986, BAT, as reported by *The* (Newark) *Star-Ledger* "...helps old-time players who have run out of money or who need special attention for other problems. Mr. Black said, 'We do it quietly because, if we didn't, they wouldn't let us help. They are a proud bunch.' Mr. Black would visit ballparks to talk to players about the emotional and financial aspects of 'life after baseball.' "

There was an appreciation dinner sponsored by BAT posthumously honoring Joe Black held on February 27, 2003. Former Red Sox and Tigers pitcher Earl Wilson was the President and CEO of BAT at the time. He wrote on the program that "Trying to walk in Joe Black's shoes is impossible, not only because they were large ones but because no one could ever fill them the way he did, with that ever-purposeful stride and ever-present smile." Mr. Wilson and all others associated with BAT expressed their sadness at the death of Joe Black. Mr. Wilson went on, "As a member of the Board of Directors of BAT, and a Vice President until his death, Joe Black would educate those on the Board to the plight of the players from the Negro Leagues, the Minor Leagues, and the Professional Women's Baseball League. He was an important voice, and his advocacy of overlooked and underserved groups was deeply appreciated by his fellow Directors on the Board."

Joe and Joe served long and hard to help down-and-out former players and their families, including Negro leagues players. Joe Garagiola relates a story in which Joe Black was trying through BAT to help a widow of a Negro league player. She needed funds and was convinced that she should refinance her house. Joe Black recommended against it and told her she could solve the financial problem without a new loan on her house. Nevertheless, she went ahead. Joe Black, instead of writing her off for not listening, hung in there with her. A couple wanted to move into the house with her and demanded power of attorney from the elderly lady. Joe stepped in and strongly opposed this loss of legal authority. This time she heeded his advice. Fellow Dodger pitcher Don Newcombe said that "Joe was tenacious and inspirational."

According to Joe Garagiola, Joe always tried to give a voice to the vulnerable. Former National League president Len Coleman remembers that Joe devoted a great deal of time and attention to helping bona fide players of the old Negro leagues, as well as their families. They needed to show that they were responsible people before help would be given. Joe Black believed deeply in personal responsibility.

The executive director of BAT, Jim Martin, got to know Joe. He commented, "Joe was a very caring guy. He was very heavily involved with the Negro League players. He tried to help them out and was instrumental in having them receive some kind of pension from Major League Baseball."

Former players who have or are currently serving on the BAT Board of Directors include Bobby Murcer, Steve Garvey, Bob Gibson, Joe Morgan, Robin Roberts, Jim Palmer, Ralph Branca, Joe Pignatano, Lou Johnson, Ted Sizemore, Frank Torre, Bobby Valentine, Greg Wilcox, and Randy Winn. On the Advisory Board are or have been Jay Bell, Carl Erskine, Whitey Ford, Joe Girardi, Sandy Koufax, Willie Mays, Warren Spahn, and Don Zimmer.

The Baseball Assistance Team is also involved in the community with the Roberto Clemente Award, Boys and Girls Clubs of America, and many other groups, including the Jackie Robinson Foundation. Joe served on the Foundation, whose present chairman is Joe's good friend, former National League president Len Coleman.

Chapter 21
Joe Garagiola and Joe Black

At one time they were competitors. In Joe Black's rookie year, he was a dominating pitcher. That year of 1952 Joe Garagiola was catching for the Pittsburgh Pirates after being traded from the St. Louis Cardinals. As mentioned, Garagiola batted around .270 that year but he hit .360 against Joe Black. Later, after they became close friends, they would laugh about it.

They were such good friends that Joe Garagiola led the first Memorial Celebration held in honor of Joe Black in May 2002. This one was in Phoenix, where he resided after retiring from Greyhound. Aside from the family, Mr. Jerry Reinsdorf was the only person who attended both tributes, Arizona and New Jersey. According to Ms. Martha Jo Black, Mr. Garagiola was so choked up he could barely deliver his words about her father. It was an uncharacteristic moment for the gregarious man who was never at a loss for words. Even when he does commentary for the Westminster Dog Show from Madison Square Garden, Joe Garagiola always has something to say. He was simply overcome at the loss of his great, long-term friend, Mr. Joe Black.

Like many others, Garagiola respected Joe Black's sense of fairness. He saw his friend as a person with real integrity and compassion, qualities Garagiola had a reputation for possessing himself. After a career of nine years as a journeyman catcher in the major leagues, he was offered a job with the St. Louis Cardinals broadcasting team. He went on to earn Sportscasters Hall of Fame honors by broadcasting the All-Star Game and World Series for NBC-TV and later the New York Yankee telecasts, working with Phil Rizzuto, Red Barber, and Jerry Coleman.

Joe Garagiola was a host of NBC's *Today* show for eleven years. He had his friend Joe Black on once and said he was a hit. Both men possessed big hearts. In 1991, Mr. Garagiola won the prestigious Ford C. Frick Award, named after the former Commissioner and given annually to a broadcaster who has made major contributions to the sport of baseball. He loved the game, was involved with BAT, and was always a knowledgeable, humorous, and interesting broadcaster. He was well known for his famous quips. One of my favorites: "The 1952 Pirates lost 112 (of 154) games. One day we had a rainout and we staged a victory party."

During his career as a ballplayer and for twenty years thereafter, Joe Garagiola had a problem that troubled him greatly. It was during this time that his friendship with Joe Black was solidified. The situation arose in a game between the Brooklyn Dodgers and St. Louis Cardinals, played in St. Louis in 1950. Joe Black was not yet with the Dodgers at this time.

Jackie Robinson was playing first base for the Dodgers. Cardinal catcher Joe Garagiola hit a ground ball and ran to first base. When Garagiola reached the bag, he found Robinson's foot pretty much covering it. As he stepped down, he nicked Jackie's shoe while crossing first base. Umpire Beans Reardon asked Jackie if he was all right. Jackie replied, "Yes, no thanks to him," while looking at Joe. Later in that same game, St. Louis star outfielder Enos Slaughter spiked Robinson high on the shin, causing bleeding. The next day in newspapers all over the country there was a story about how Joe Garagiola had viciously spiked Jackie Robinson. The facts were confused and stayed that way.

That story had legs. Despite the constant denials by Garagiola, the story was repeated endlessly. The pictures showed that it was #9 (Slaughter) and not #17 (Garagiola), but it did not seem to matter. Even famed sportswriter Maury Allen perpetuated the story of Garagiola spiking Jackie.

This tale of unsportsmanlike conduct went on for years, with Joe Garagiola, a clean player, suffering from its effects. It became so bad that kids wrote letters to Mr. Garagiola asking why he did that to Jackie Robinson, after Betsy Bale Lord, a popular children's author, wrote the story in a book. After that, even Joe's own granddaughter questioned him. The affable and kind ballplayer turned sportscaster and media person was haunted by this false tale.

When Joe Black joined the Dodgers in 1952, he heard the story. As was his nature, he wanted to be fair so he asked Garagiola about it and learned what he believed was the truth after checking the facts. He then consistently stood up for Joe Garagiola whenever the old story surfaced. Joe greatly appreciated Joe for his fairness and integrity, and their friendship deepened.

When Joe Black vouched for Joe Garagiola, he had excellent credibility as the former roommate of Jackie Robinson. Since fairness, truth, and justice were so important to him, Joe Black tried to set the record straight but the story had developed a life of its own. It was not until a sports roundtable discussion at Hofstra University twenty years after the incident that Enos Slaughter finally admitted that he was the one. Joe Black actually telephoned his friend from that room and told him the good news. Then, Ken Burns got it right in his storied PBS baseball series. Enos Slaughter was cited as the player who viciously spiked Jackie Robinson in that game. Joe Garagiola was finally off the hook. It had taken a long time for the truth to come out.

Later, Joe and Joe gave a talk about fairness at a school in Phoenix. This story was the example they used.

Some considerable time after the admission, the salty Enos Slaughter was interviewed by television talk show host Larry King who noted that Slaughter was from Arkansas, had never played with or against a black player, and had bitter feelings about blacks entering the big leagues. Slaughter described the incident as follows:

"The first year Jackie came up he was playing first base. I hit a ground ball to second base and I beat out the hit and deliberately stepped on Robinson's ankle, drawing blood. I knew he wouldn't say anything because his first two years of playing he couldn't retaliate at all. So I got to second and kind of smugly stared him down.

Two years later, I'm at Ebbets Field and Robinson's playing second base. I hit a ball off the right-field wall. I'm heading into second base which Robinson is covering. The ball is thrown into him and he takes the ball and slams me in the mouth with it, knocking out four teeth. I was spitting blood all over the place. He looked into my eyes and said, "I never forget." That son-of-a-bitch had my respect for the rest of my days."

Joe Garagiola treasured his friend Joe Black. He noted that Joe Black was never bitter about losing all those prime years in the Negro leagues instead of playing in the majors. He was always above the fray. His friend never judged people on their wallet or their fame. He truly believed you should love thy neighbor.

When Joe Black worked for Major League Baseball after his retirement from Greyhound, he advised players to save their money, get an education, avoid being conned, and always act respectfully—including donating to BAT to help those who came before the big money and the large pensions. He told players they are accountable for all of their actions. Ken Griffey Jr. and others were drawn to the wisdom and genuine sincerity of Joe Black. In fact, Joe Black was known for his words of wisdom. He always wanted to help and, according to Dusty Baker, "did not seek credit or accolades."

According to Garagiola, Joe Black always performed to the maximum and beyond on any job he held. He reshaped the community relations program of the Arizona Diamondbacks when working for them. He was the antithesis of a "token black" when serving as a Greyhound executive in the transportation industry. He played baseball intelligently and well while ignoring the racial taunts such as "Old Black Joe," which he heard often. He taught, spoke, wrote, advised, and mentored with all his heart, whether it was students, old ballplayers and their families, modern major leaguers, the public, or his own family.

In the words of Joe Garagiola, a man known for his way with words, "If heaven is home plate, Joe is safe at home."

Chapter 22
Continuing Education for Us

Our former teacher always encouraged us to seek more education and training, and he followed our progress. He talked to us about thinking right. He knew I was interested in a career in law, and he encouraged me by telling me what a noble profession it was. Mr. Black then told me he was proud of my accomplishments and trusted that I would be a good lawyer with a heart. It was during that conversation that he said to me that I should call him "Joe" from now on. It felt odd but I did it. Later, it felt more natural. I saw it as an honor and realized that he had now gone from teacher to mentor.

It was a marvel to me that my former teacher who was such a busy man would make sure we stayed in touch. One day, Joe called me at work to tell me he would be in D.C. in a week for the Congressional Black Caucus meetings. He knew I had recently gotten married and invited my wife Adrianne and me to brunch on Sunday morning at the Washington Hilton. I told him that sounded great. I was really looking forward to Adrianne meeting Joe. She was pleased, because she knew how important he was to me.

On Sunday morning we got a little bit of a late start. I suggested to Adrianne that I drop her off while I parked the car. She could then go and meet up with Joe. I had not considered that she had never met him before.

Adrianne only knew that Joe was a large black man who would probably be dressed for the meetings he would be attending later. Unfortunately, my wife grew up in a prissy, lily-white New England town with no black families living there at all so when she stepped into the Hilton lobby and saw many large black men, most in business suits, she was taken aback.

Adrianne related that a very large black man in a golf sweater and pants approached her and asked, "Are you looking for me?"

She quickly responded in a knee-jerk way, "No."

He walked away. I was still parking the car when the same man approached, and smiling, he said, "Are you sure you're not looking for me?"

Again she curtly replied, "No."

I then walked into the lobby where I spotted Joe and greeted him. "Joe, it's great to see you. Thanks for inviting us."

We walked over to where my embarrassed wife was standing. Her face was red and she immediately apologized. Joe's response was kind.

"Don't worry about it. If I were you and a large black man like me approached asking if you're looking for him, I would act the same way you did."

We laughed and went on to a very enjoyable brunch. It was wonderful to see the interaction between Joe and Adrianne. He went out of his way to make her feel comfortable. She eventually got to know him to the point where Adrianne and I, along with our sons, Ethan and Elliott, visited Joe and Martha Jo one Christmas at their home in Phoenix. I was so glad to expose my family to my mentor. I knew my boys would benefit from his sage words. The words of Dusty Baker seem apropos: "Joe Black was unique in that he transcended all generations and societies."

An added bonus of the visit was seeing the apple of her father's eye, Martha Jo. Joe had fought for and received custody of Martha Jo when she was six years old. Martha Jo, in an article in *Morgan* magazine in fall of 2002, after the death of her father, related, "My father won custody of me and raised me by himself. My father did everything from braiding my hair to talking about sex education, to making sure I studied, to teaching me regarding saving money."

When Joe invited our family to join him at the All-Star Game in Baltimore in 1993, he showed our boys a good time, taking them down on the field as he had done with our Hubbard team. We then had a long, leisurely meal with him and met many luminaries such as Joe Garagiola, Larry Doby, and Donald Fehr, head of the players' union. During our dinner, which lasted several hours, I particularly wanted my boys to hear the pearls of wisdom that came from Joe. He did not disappoint. He emphasized the importance of an education no matter what your job, including baseball player. He discussed the quality of being truthful and developing a good reputation. My family was always richer for the experience of being with Mr. Joe Black.

At the end of the meal, the server asked us if we would like dessert. None of us had room except for Joe. After his playing days, and particularly after his Greyhound retirement, he ballooned in weight. He said that sweets were a weakness that he could not give up. He enjoyed a generous piece of chocolate layer cake as he continued to talk to us about things that count, particularly to young men. I noticed that our two boys were spellbound as they took in his words. He was so intelligent, honest, and humorous, all at the same time, that we were all enamored.

Joe's vice was food, particularly sweets. He called Jerry Reinsdorf about going to lunch one day. Jerry picked up the phone to the usual question: "Are we going to eat healthy or good?" Mr. Reinsdorf said he would prefer healthy so they went to a restaurant that featured an extensive salad bar. After they had consumed large salads, Joe got up from the table, telling Jerry he would be right back. It seems that Joe found out that for the price they had paid, they were entitled to go into another buffet line in the back room—the pasta bar. Within minutes, he returned with a heaping helping for both of them. Jerry declined. Healthy or good?

Former National League President Len Coleman recalled the time he, Joe, and their good friend Frank Robinson attended a game together. Joe announced to his friends that he was on a diet and would not be eating the ballpark food at the game. A few innings into the game, Len and Frank caught Joe hiding the Cracker Jacks in the seat. He had a sheepish grin on his face when they were discovered.

Frank Robinson and Joe also appeared on *The Cosby Show* as special guests along with their good friend. There was also a television video called "*The Boys of Summer*" that featured Joe. He always made an impression and his character would shine through. Joe Black would help everyone to the best of his abilities, which were considerable.

Chapter 23
Mentor/Mentee—The New Relationship

A family man, corporate executive, newspaper columnist, radio commentator, and *Ebony* magazine columnist, Joe still managed to contact his old students from his teaching days. One day I opened the mail to find that he had sent me our Hubbard Junior High School team picture, which appears as a part of this book. It hangs in my law office in Rockville, Maryland.

I was so thrilled to be getting continuing advice and support from the man I most respected, with the exception of my father, who passed away after I had finished law school. Joe Black was a great listener who would guide me on making key decisions. It bothered me that he asked nothing for himself, so I was pleased when he called to ask me to look out for his niece, Bridgette Greer, Esq., who was going to be a new lawyer with the Prince George's County Attorney's Office in the contiguous county to mine. He was very proud of his niece, who had made the most of her education. He loved and was very proud of his children—son Chico and daughter Martha Jo.

At the end of my first year in my private law practice, I received a call from Joe. He was at the peak of his career as the first black executive in the transportation business. He caught me on a rare day when I was little down. Although I tried to hide it from him, Joe sensed my mood and drew me out. I told him I had worked hard the last year but had made very little money. Fortunately, my wife had a good job. In those days, you could not advertise, there was no Internet, and work was slow. I relied mostly on cases rejected by the older lawyer in the suite. I was impatient with the finances but happy with the results I had achieved for my clients—there just were not enough clients. I told Joe I could have made some more money if I had bent my ethics. We both knew I would not do that. I apologized for my somber mood and asked how he was doing. My mood was about to change due to my mentor.

The next thing I knew, I received a telephone call from Joe's administrative aide at Greyhound in Phoenix. I was invited to participate in an upcoming event, "D.C. Salutes Joe Black Night," to be held in the spring of 1976 at the downtown Statler Hilton. It would be in celebration of his character and all the good he had done. I gladly accepted. It was an honor to be invited to speak.

When the big night came, I rented my tux and went downtown with my wife. Optimistically, I loaded my suit pockets with several hundred business cards much to the disapproval of my wife. We entered the elegant hotel ballroom not knowing what to expect. The large room had more than one hundred large tables set up with an elevated dais at the front of the room. An attractive group of people, mostly black, took their seats. My wife was welcomed to her table in a friendly manner and I was directed to the head table. We were early so I was the first one seated. Soon the table was fully occupied.

I turned to my left and introduced myself to Mr. Jesse Owens, the famous Olympian who won at the 1936 Berlin games, much to Hitler's dismay. This sports immortal was extremely cordial and thought it was interesting that I had been a student of his friend Joe Black. Immediately to my right was Don Newcombe, a star Dodger pitcher. Seated between these two celebrities, I was pinching myself. The mayor of the District of Columbia at that time, the Honorable Walter Washington, was present. I even got to say hello to Mr. John Pepe of Plainfield High wrestling fame. I still remembered how he flipped Mr. Black in gym class. Bam! Joe Black valued his relationships from every part of his life and worked hard to maintain them.

The guest of honor arrived with his children, Chico and Martha Jo. He went down the line greeting everyone. Some of the famous people at the head table gave humorous, laudatory speeches. Joe introduced me before my short speech. Here is what he said: "Now, everyone, I want you to meet Steve Selzer. Steve was my student at Hubbard Junior High in our hometown of Plainfield, New Jersey, when I was a teacher there." Then, the honoree addressed the large audience in a louder voice: "Steve Selzer is now an attorney in Rockville, Maryland." He was so emphatic that we all just stopped for a moment.

A little bit stunned by Joe's introduction, I rose to shake his hand as the large audience applauded, seemingly respectful of our relationship. I then was able to talk about the character education (including "Happy Hour") that we students had received from our teacher, who emphasized the importance of education, fairness, and respect. Since I am a lawyer, I like to talk, and I related the Louie Pompano story to the audience, which they seemed to appreciate. Maybe I was able to give Joe Black's friends and admirers an added perspective about the man we were there to honor. I was so glad for this opportunity. Little did I realize the effect it would have on my legal career.

On Monday morning I went to my law office. It looked as if it would be a pretty quiet day. Instead, the phone rang off the hook with guests of the salute and their friends and relatives calling. I am grateful that the phone has not stopped since. I thanked my mentor and I remain very grateful to this day. Joe set out to do it and created the tipping point in my legal career, which has now spanned over thirty years. He had helped his student, which was his goal. I found myself in the halo of his fine reputation. Clients actually told me, "If you're good enough for Joe, you're good enough for me."

Chapter 24
Lessons Remembered and Applied

The 1997 World Series between the Cleveland Indians and the Florida Marlins was very exciting, going a full seven games. Game 7 was played in Miami as the Marlins, in only their fifth season of operation, tried to win their first World Series. The Indians were in their second World Series in three years and had star rookie pitcher Jaret Wright on the mound. He had shut out the Marlins for six innings, while the Indians had scored two runs.

In the seventh inning, Bobby Bonilla was facing the unhittable Wright. After missing two pitches, Bonilla walked behind home plate to the box, where National League President Len Coleman was sitting with a guest. The ever-observant Bob Costas, who was broadcasting the game on NBC, followed Bonilla. Suddenly the exuberant Costas belted out, "Bobby Bonilla is talking to the old Dodger pitcher, Joe Black, who is sitting in the box with Mr. Coleman. Bonilla has just nodded his head and is returning to the plate."

What happened next is part of baseball history. On the very next pitch, Bobby Bonilla hit a gigantic home run off Wright, which changed the game's momentum. The Marlins went on to win Game 7 and the World Series.

What happened when Bonilla had his short talk with the seventy-three-year-old former Dodger pitcher? It just so happens that I know. I heard it from a very good source. Joe Black summoned up a memory from forty-five years before, which he felt applied to the situation at hand. He told Bonilla that he was throwing fastballs, like Wright was, to Mickey Mantle in the seventh game of the 1952 World Series with great success. Then, Mantle stepped out of the batter's box for a minute. When he stepped back in, he stepped one foot further back in the box. That adjustment allowed Mantle to catch up with the next pitch which he hit for a titanic home run. Both Mantle and Bonilla were powerful switch-hitters batting against right-handed pitchers from the left side. In just two minutes the old veteran was able to convey the lesson to Bonilla. It is already part of baseball legend. From then on, Joe's close friend Len Coleman had a lot of fun introducing Joe to others as the "National League hitting coach."

How is that for learning and remembering a lesson and then applying it correctly? Joe Black was purported to have an encyclopedic recall of everything baseball. He was a man who prized the human ability to learn and to reason. That is why it was such a privilege to be his student and mentee. All who came in contact with him—whether personally, by newspaper, or by radio or television—were touched in a positive way. He was a strong family man interested in helping others by teaching, including character education, coaching, encouraging young people to act right and respectfully, and setting the example with his own ethical conduct. Whether you call it "character" or "ethics," Joe Black believed in teaching his values both as an educator and a businessman because he knew how important it was to individuals, schools, families, communities, the workplace, and our country.

Joe Black built self-esteem in others, as his mother had done with him by repeatedly saying, "Ain't nobody better than you." Joe Black looked out for the underdog. He assisted others in finding their courage. He valued his education and helped and encouraged many others to seek theirs. He was a stellar corporate executive with Greyhound Corporation and always a civil human being. He knew many famous people and regular folk and treated them all the same—with respect and dignity.

The day that our lives crossed was truly one of the luckiest days of my life. I am aware that it was a very unusual occurrence for Joe Black to become my mentor, and I am genuinely grateful. I share our story and the goodness of Joe Black so that others may benefit.

Chapter 25
The Memorial Celebration of a Great Man

The day was June 1, 2002. My wife and I were greeted by Joe Black's niece, Bridgette Greer, at the entrance to the old, beautiful, spacious Mount Olive Baptist Church, not far from the railroad tracks in Plainfield, New Jersey. From the front of the church, I could see what had been my father's old auto body shop and yard. Bridgette took us to the front row to be seated since I would be the first speaker. As we sat down in the crowded church, the man next to me extended his hand. I shook it and then looked up at his face. It was Bill Cosby.

Joe had never dropped names so I did not know they were great friends until I saw Mr. Cosby sitting there in deep, respectful thought. Later, Joe's daughter, Martha Jo, told me how close they were. Her "Uncle Bill" had even babysat her. It did not surprise me. Both were great educators. Both were generous givers. Each had a clean sense of humor. It occurred to me that I had seen Joe, along with Frank Robinson, make a guest appearance on *The Cosby Show*. On March 2, 2007, while being inducted into the NAACP Hall of Fame at the 2007 NAACP Awards on national television, Dr. Bill Cosby paid his respects once more to his friend, Mr. Joe Black, by speaking of their poignant final conversation before Joe's passing, as he does in the foreword to this book.

This magnificent church that the Black family had attended for years was packed with people. Still getting oriented, I looked just past my wife and saw a familiar face. The program confirmed that it was Jerry Reinsdorf, chairman of the Chicago White Sox and Chicago Bulls, who would speak second. Mr. Reinsdorf, with a reputation as a hard-nosed businessman, spoke of his close relationship with Joe, breaking down twice during his speech. In fact, the audience was full of humanity—famous people and not-so-famous people, people of all races, ages, and backgrounds, all there to pay tribute to Mr. Joe Black, a man who had helped many people and touched many lives.

A member of the family introduced me to the audience as his former student, and I went to the podium. I had given my wife the notes I had prepared because I knew they were unnecessary. I could speak straight from the heart about my teacher and mentor, Mr. Joe Black. He had passed away at age seventy-eight of prostate cancer in Phoenix, where he lived, on May 17, 2002. There had been a funeral and a memorial celebration in Phoenix, and now, on June 1, 2002, there would be this memorial celebrating his life and honoring him in his home town at his family's church. It was my honor to be invited to speak.

As I looked out over the crowd, I saw an old Dodger, Don Zimmer, among others. There were former teachers, sports figures, and many community and church members. It was standing room only. On the other side of the stage, there were large stand-up photos of Joe Black with Jackie Robinson, Roberto Clemente, Ken Griffey Jr., John H. Johnson, CEO John W. Teets of Greyhound Corporation, Joe Garagiola, and Joseph (Chico) Black and Martha Jo Black, his son and daughter.

When it was my turn to speak, I spoke of how Mr. Black had chosen to become a teacher after his major league career and how fortunate

I had been as a seventh grader at Hubbard Junior High School. He was a caring teacher who encouraged learning and discussed values such as integrity and respect. He was revered for his character, and he taught character in class and by example. Then, later in life, he became my mentor. Mr. Black gladly helped me and other former students to move ahead in our careers. I was able to relate some humorous and hopefully meaningful stories that demonstrated how he stressed education and used clever techniques to discipline his students and coach his junior high baseball players. Mr. Black was a true character education teacher.

I don't mean to boast but my wife later told me that Bill Cosby was slapping his knee when he heard the funny anecdotes in the context of education about his good friend of many years. Mr. Cosby is a great believer in education—he even holds a doctorate degree in the subject—and Mr. Black was a fine and respected public school teacher for seven years. Bill Cosby whispered to me after I finished to a fine ovation and sat back down next to him, "Too many jokes." I didn't know exactly what he meant, but humor was a great part of Mr. Black's personality even as he emphasized important values and lessons. I had chosen my stories carefully, and I believe they reflected the tact and good taste of my teacher and mentor. I finished my speech by saying, "I was so lucky to have known him."

When I ended my speech at the church by saying that it had been my good fortune and great privilege to know this extraordinary person, I was speaking from the heart. I was a lucky boy, then man, that our paths had crossed and re-crossed. Mr. Joe Black was my teacher and then my mentor. He always wanted to help me at all stages, and there was nothing I could do to repay the debt except to thank him privately. And so it was a great honor to speak publicly at this memorial celebration of his meaningful and distinguished life.

As we were leaving the memorial, I went out into the sunlight. As my eyes were still adjusting, I saw a legendary person walking toward me. He shook my hand and graciously said, "Mr. Selzer, you really captured Joe."

"Thank you," I replied. Then I heard myself say, "Adrianne Selzer, I would like you to meet Sandy Koufax." As they shook hands, I realized that I was talking to my all-time childhood sports hero.

Once I had recovered enough, I asked how he and Joe were friends. I did not think their careers overlapped. Koufax said, "It was in 1955 that I was signed as a bonus baby by the Dodgers. I was just a kid, but the rule was that I had to replace a veteran on the roster as a bonus baby. Because of the bonus check I received, and the rule, I was shunned by every player on the team except one. Joe Black came over to me, put his arm around me, and said, 'Come on, kid. I'll show you the ropes.' We became great friends for life even though Joe was traded to Cincinnati in the middle of the season. He was there for me in my time of need." The legendary, reclusive pitcher made sure he attended the memorial celebration. Loyalty was important to both men.

A further illustration of their friendship occurred in the summer of 1965. According to Jane Leavy in her book, simply called *Sandy Koufax*, she spoke to Joe who told her:

"The Dodgers were in New York to play the Mets. Black was out of baseball and working as a vice president for the Greyhound Corporation. Joe related, "I'm just walking on Fifth Avenue, y'know, and all of a sudden two hands go over my eyes. I'm like, what the?" Someone says, "Guess who?"

I turned around and it was Sandy Koufax. I said, 'Where did you come from?' He was across the street, walking in the opposite direction.

He ran all the way to come my way. That's when he was a star. I was a hacker, a one-year wonder. Here's a man who says, 'You're my friend then, you're my friend now,' the same old Sandy Koufax."[x]

Joe Black, with his unselfish attitude and enjoyment of people, had many meaningful long-term relationships. One of these relationships was with the outstanding ballplayer and manager Dusty Baker, who described Joe Black in this way: "He was one of the best, most fair, and strongest men that I knew. Whenever you had a problem he knew to call you. I may not have talked to him for three months and I needed to talk to someone and there he was. It was like instinct with Joe. He always had the right answers. He was so giving of himself."

I have always believed that life is about relationships. Here I was crossing all these paths because of my relationship to Joe Black. I benefitted tremendously from a man who was very different from me. I grew up in a comfortable home in a middle class white neighborhood. I was a pesky seventh-grade adolescent when we met. I never would have guessed what would happen.

I was so lucky to have known him.

Author's Notes

The author wishes to thank Martha Jo and Joseph "Chico" Black, the daughter and son of Joe Black, for their permission to quote from their father's 1983 self-published autobiography, *Ain't Nobody Better than You*. Unless otherwise noted, all quotes from Joe Black are from that book.

The author would like to thank the Black family—Martha Jo, Chico, and Joe's sister, Phyllis Greer, for the use of the photographs in this book.

Endnotes

Chapter 5

i.   Larry Lester, *Baseball's National Showcase* (University of Nebraska Press, 2002).

Chapter 7

ii.   Arnold Ampersad, Jackie Robinson (Ballantine Books, 1998).

Chapter 8

iii.   Thomas Oliphant, *Praying for Gil Hodges* (Thomas Dunn Books, 2005).

iv.   Larry King, *Why I Love Baseball* (Phoenix Books, 2004).

v.   Peter Golenbock, *Bums: An Oral History of the Brooklyn Dodgers* (Contemporary Books, 1984)

vi.   Roger Kahn, *The Boys of Summer* (Harper & Row, 1972)

Chapter 10

vii.   Steven Michael Selzer, *By George! Mr. Washington's Guide to Civility Today* (Andrews McMeel, 2000).

Chapter 13

viii.   Steven Covey, *Everyday Greatness* (Thomas Nelson Publishers, 2006).

Chapter 17

ix.   Roy Campanella, *It's Good to be Alive* (Little Brown and Company, 1959).

Chapter 25

x.   Jane Leavy, *Sandy Koufax* (HarperCollins, 2002).

Acknowledgments

The writing of this book emanated from the heart. It is my intention to honor a great man who lived a life of giving to others in many ways. Now, hopefully, more people can benefit from his sage advice and the inspiring and motivating lessons of his life. Posthumously, this man of many attributes who engendered enormous respect can still help others. To those of us who were fortunate enough to have known him, that was and continues to be its own reward.

Many others helped me in various ways in writing this book. As acts of love, the family generously provided me with photos, articles, mementos, and stories. I am very thankful to Joe's daughter, Martha Jo Black, and his son, Joseph "Chico" Black, Jr, his sister Phyllis and niece Bridgette Greer. Martha reached inside and wrote the meaningful Introduction.

Friends of Joe provided me with many wonderful stories about a man they loved. Among them are Jerry Reinsdorf, Dusty Baker, Len Coleman, Joe Garagiola, Sandy Koufax, Earl Wilson, and Jerry Colangelo. Attorney George Simms was nice enough to tell me how he was positively influenced by this man he had never met. Bill Cosby contributed the fine Foreword in this book about his "big brother."

Additionally, I would like to thank Colleen Greer, Joy Ceesay, and, especially, Jenn Cadiz for guiding me through the process of producing this book. Lastly, I want to express appreciation to my family—my wife, Adrianne, my sons Ethan and Elliott, and my daughter-in-law, Natalie. Our sweet dog, Chancellor, showed great patience while I was banging on the keys and not able to pet him at the same time.